The
Happiness
Paradox

FAMILIUS

Published by Familius LLC, www.familius.com

Familius books are available at special discounts for bulk purchases, whether for sales promotions or for family or corporate use. For more information, contact Premium Sales at 801-552-7298 or email orders@familius.com

Library of Congress Catalog-in-Publication Data
2018945275
pISBN 9781641700535
eISBN 9781641701044

Printed in the United States of America

Edited by Michele Robbins, Peg Sandkam, and Alison Strobel
Cover and book design by David Miles

10 9 8 7 6 5 4 3 2 1

First Edition

Richard Eyre

THE VERY THINGS
WE THOUGHT WOULD
BRING US JOY
ACTUALLY STEAL IT AWAY

The
Happiness
Paradox

CONTENTS

FOREWORD

BY STEPHEN M. R. COVEY

I think what my good friend Richard Eyre has wonderfully done here in this creative and insightful book is to get to the very essence of happiness—to the fact that how happy we are is inexorably connected to what we are seeking. Indeed, true joy cannot come to us, at least not consistently, if we are seeking the wrong things.

Thus, the key to more happiness lies not so much in what we have or even in what we do, but in how we think—in the paradigms of our mind and in the desires of our hearts.

Part of maturing or growing up is learning to control ourselves and our emotions and behavior, learning to take responsibility for ourselves and for what we own, and learning to be independent in our thinking and self-reliant in our personal lives. And there is a degree of happiness in learning and practicing these things.

The question is whether there is a higher level of thinking and of living that brings with it a higher level of happiness.

Richard says that there is. He teaches us that once we have learned the lessons of control, ownership, and independence we can move beyond these useful but flawed frameworks and find a higher, truer way of thinking about ourselves and about our lives. I will let you discover these higher paradigms in the other side of this book.

I will just preview that these higher paradigms both derive from and produce trust in all its forms, including self-trust and relationship trust. And as my life's work has been about trust, I have found that the connection of trust to happiness is overwhelming. As I've worked with people and leaders all over the world, people will often use the word "joy" in describing the high-trust relationships in their lives. Plus, you can see it—or the lack of it—in their faces. At the core of strong and enduring relationships is trust, while the very definition of a bad relationship is "little or no trust." I assert that trust both underlies and derives from these alternative attitudes Richard discusses.

I wish to conclude this brief foreword with a short personal story about this book's tremendous author. When I was a college student, I came across a book that had two front covers—that had to be turned upside down and read from both sides. It was a book called, on one side, *I Challenge You* and, on the other side, *I Promise You*. Readers who were more drawn to challenges could read from that side and turn the book over to read the promise that went with each challenge, and readers who were more interested in promises could start there and flip the book upside down to see what they had to do to get the thing that was promised. The book was original and creative, and it impacted my life.

That book was coauthored by a young writer named Richard Eyre, who later shifted his emphasis to writing about family and parenting and life-balance—and become a *New York Times* #1 bestselling author in the process.

I am personally pleased that, all these decades later, Richard has written another double-cover book, and that this one is in some ways an advanced edition of the first one—a challenge to reinvent our paradigms and our priorities, and a promise of a higher kind of happiness if we do.

— **STEPHEN M. R. COVEY**

New York Times and # 1 *Wall Street Journal–*
bestselling author of *The Speed of Trust*

For my children—Saren, Shawni, Josh,
Saydi, Jonah, Talmadge, Noah, Eli, and
Charity—who I *love more* every day; and
each of whom has managed to pass
through the phases of control, ownership,
and independence faster than I did.

All royalties from this book go
to Eyrealm, a public charity that
helps children and families in
developing countries.

par·a·dox
A contradiction or incongruity; a result
that is backward from what we expected.

Can we unwind some of the illusions and
inaccurate assumptions that are keeping us
from happiness?

The distorted lens of **OWNERSHIP**
causes us to perceive the world as a competition,
to constantly compare and judge,
and to develop the habits of selfishness.

The mistaken notion of **INDEPENDENCE**
puts us alone against the world
and develops a brittle facade of pride
which hides the vulnerability that could help us
to better love and be loved.

The presumptuous perspective of **CONTROL**
makes us swim against the flow of opportunities
and become less sensitive to others
even as it deprives us of both faith and spontaneity.

Why then, are these the three things
that all of us seem to be seeking?
Why indeed!

PREFACE

PREMISE . . .

The premise is this: We started with joy. We all began life with our default switches set to happiness. As babies, except when something (hunger, thirst, a little tummy ache, or a wet diaper) distracted us, our natural state was joy. We were easy to delight. We smiled often and laughed—even giggled—a lot. People around us liked to make us happy, and our happiness made them happy. We were not self-conscious about our happiness. We waived our arms. We squealed.

But as we gradually grew older, that happiness began to ebb.

We started growing away from joy as we tacked on the years. By the time we were in kindergarten, while happiness was still our modus operandi, there were more and more things that pulled us away from it. As we went through elementary school we began to learn the concept of ownership, and with it came selfishness and competition. We began to learn the notion of control, and with it came pride and frustration. We began to learn the concept of independence, and with it came loneliness and isolation.

These concepts were taught to us by adults, who also served as the examples of them.

The premise is that ownership, control, and independence are essentially economic terms, and that when they are applied too broadly and adopted too comprehensively, they become our deceivers. They become the three thieves of our joy.

But remember that happiness is our natural state. We don't have to discover happiness; we merely need to recover it.

And we can recover it by grasping, exposing, and discarding three of the things that have sucked happiness away from us. We can come to understand the limitations and illusions and deceptions of control, ownership, and independence which combine, intertwine, and cocoon us into a place where we are confined and walled off from our natural state of joy.

The premise is that our pursuit of control, ownership, and independence is keeping us from the rest, the peace, the natural world, and the spontaneity that go into joy, even as that pursuit creates the pressure, the tension and stress, and the comparing and competing that bring unhappiness.

The premise is that we can recover our birthright of joy by exposing and incarcerating the three joy thieves, banning them from our brains, and adopting in their place three alternative attitudes, paradigms, viewpoints, or approaches to life that absorb rather than attack joy, that prompt rather than prevent happiness.

The premise is that happiness is less about our external circumstances and more about our internal paradigms—less about what happens to us and more about what happens in us.

Don't misunderstand, this is not a book about positive mental attitude or about simply deciding to be happy. Rather it is about changing how we see the world around us—changing the lens through which we

see our lives and our circumstances and ourselves and literally turning
upside down our notions of what we want and how we want to live.

The premise is that happiness and joy are not synonyms, but rather compatible and complementary elements that can each be pursued and that can rub off on each other.

Happiness is a momentary, fleeting emotion that is largely dependent on the situation. Joy is an enduring, progressing state of mind that gradually rises above circumstances.

Happiness is associated with pleasure, with good fortune, and with achievement. Joy is linked to responsibility, to sacrifice, and to relationships.

Happiness depends somewhat on health, wealth, and freedom from pain and confinement. Joy stems from awareness and perspective, and freedom from error and arrogance.

Happiness connects to confidence, comfort, and getting—and brings with it excitement. Joy incorporates humility, awe, and giving—and brings with it peace.

But they are not opponents; they are teammates. They don't compete; they collaborate. And they are both worthy of pursuit. They are both the right things to want, to desire, and to strive for. In fact, they are so related that they should be thought of as one thing with two parts.

And the reason they (or it) are so elusive and hard to find is not that they are vague or difficult to identify or to recognize, and it's not that they are the wrong thing to pursue; it is that we are looking for them in the wrong places and letting their counterfeits lead us down the wrong paths.

The premise is that it is possible to pursue and achieve both the Western notion of seeking and finding joy *and* the Eastern notion of enjoying the experience now—the comgined premise is that we can en*joy* the seeking. Neither being nor becoming can get along on its own. This is not abstract as it sounds, as this book will show you. We can bridge the gap between the Western idea of finding the one individual right/best way to live and the Eastern idea of being freed from individual identity into a non-personal state of nirvana—between

the Christian idea of achieving blissful utopia or heaven and the Dharma enlightenment that reality is already complete.

So, the premise is the paradox—that the perceived control, ownership, and independence pathway is actually a diversion and a detour that leads us away rather than toward happiness and joy.

And the premise is that there is a new path, a correct one, and that path leads in rather than out—into our hearts and minds where we can reexamine who we are and what we want.

REQUEST . . .

Perhaps the first thing you noticed when you picked up this book is that it is reversible—that it has two front covers. And perhaps your first impulse was to flip the book over and find out the conclusions—to read the other side first.

Well, here is a request: Wait! Don't read side two until you have read side one.

Here's why: This side of the book is about *unlearning* three false ideas or false goals that most of us have come to accept; it is about getting rid of these three bad habits that we have developed, about exposing these attitudes that cause unhappiness, and about recognizing and overcoming obsessions we may not even know we have. I call these three goals/habits/attitudes/obsessions the *three deceivers* or the *three joy thieves*.

The flip side of this book is about three clear alternatives or new paradigms that rescue and restore joy. You must turn the book over to get to them, which makes the point that in order to move from the deceivers to the alternatives, we literally have to turn our brains and our viewpoints (and sometimes our whole lives) upside down. Or, better said, we need to turn them right side up because they have been upside down.

The three alternatives could have just followed the three deceivers as a simple linear part two of the book. But they are more dramatic than that. They are

a reversal. They are the other side. They are the flipped-over opposites of the three deceivers. They are the rescuers that regain joy from the robbers. Thus, to go from reading about one to reading about the other, you will have to turn this book over. And to go from living one to living the other, you will have to turn your life over, to literally reverse your perceptions and perspectives and paradigms from deceivers to alternatives, to shift your brain from one side to the other.

In order to move from the deceivers to the alternatives, we literally have to turn our brains and our viewpoints (and sometimes our whole lives) upside down.

What I have learned is that you have to thoroughly understand the deceivers, and why they lead away from happiness before you can discover (or even desire) the three alternatives and understand why they lead to joy.

You have to expose and discard the three joy thieves before you can appreciate the three joy rescuers or restorers.

Now all of this may sound a little oblique until you know what I am talking about, but for now, just trust me and keep the book turned the way it is now. You'll be glad you did.

Think of side one as the problem and side two as the solution.

THE START OF MY STORY: THE RIGHT GOAL BUT THE WRONG PATH

While I was a graduate student at Harvard, I became enamored with the word JOY. I came across an anonymous poem that went like this:

Happiness is a thing of here and now,
The bright leaf in the hand, the moment's sun,

The fight accomplished or the summit won.
Happiness is a lifting, buoyant kind of thing
That lifts the bird more surely on its wing.
When things go well, happiness may start,
But Joy is secret smiling of the heart.

These verses began to symbolize what I thought of as my approach to life. I began thinking of short-term happiness and longer-term joy as the goals of life—as the end to which everything else was the means.

I read whatever I could find on happiness (it was not a subject of anywhere near the intrigue and popularity it is today) and began trying to develop my own philosophy of what joy was and how to have more of it.

As our time at Harvard drew to an end, most conversations between us newly minted MBAs centered on which companies were recruiting us, how much money we could make, and how we would compete and advance in our new employment. The closest we got to deep philosophical discussions was when we speculated about what we could own and how fast we could own it. Our entire focus was about taking control of our careers, finding the most direct path to becoming the CEOs, and becoming financially independent as fast as possible.

These were heady talks, full of ambition and aggression, and they provided a certain kind of anticipatory happiness, but once in a while—in our projections of where we would be, what we would own, and how independent and in control we would be—there were tinges of anxiety and the first hints of the stress, exhaustion, and imbalance that would come with our work-oriented ambitions. For those few of us who were married, there was additional worry about statistics we had seen on the high divorce rates among MBA couples from elite universities. Were our relationships already suffering? Was the kind of achievement happiness we were intoxicated with competing with the relationship happiness we sensed was more important?

At this juncture, the questions and tradeoffs about the interrelationships of success and happiness began to occupy my thoughts.

Four years later, living outside Washington, DC, where I had cofounded a political consulting firm, I tried to capture my feelings about joy and

its pursuit in *The Discovery of Joy*, the first book I ever published. Its thesis was that there are four levels of joy: first, the physical joys of earth and body; second, the emotional joys of achievements and relationships; third, the mental joys of having a purpose and a cause; and fourth, the spiritual joy of faith. I believed that these four levels could build on each other from one to four and were best pursued in sequence. I believed anyone or everyone could discover each of them. I believed that their pursuit was the most important thing in life.

I discovered a scripture that says, "Adam fell that men might be, and men are that they might have joy." So, Adam and Eve ate that apple so they (and we) could

> **The more I observed and the more I experienced the less I understood joy and the less sure I was about how to get it.**

have joy. This may be a new dimension to the story for you, but think about it. Yes, they had to leave the garden and life was more challenging, but with the challenges came learning and progress—and joy. To me this joy seemed to define the very purpose of life.

But as life went on, and as I tried to reflect and project my life-experience on my theories of joy and of where it came from, a disturbing thing started to happen. Instead of feeling like I was understanding more about joy and learning more about its pursuit, I felt like the more I observed and the more I experienced the less I understood joy and the less sure I was about how to get it. It was a far more complex and nuanced quality than I had thought. The simple formulas for finding it and having more of it that I had offered in my book didn't seem to be working for most people. It was as though something was blocking joy no matter how deeply it was desired and how hard it was pursued. In fact, the very success and achievement that my friends were working so hard for seemed to bring more stress than happiness, and most seemed too busy to even have time to think about whether they were feeling joy at all.

By then my wife, Linda, and I had three children, and the feelings of joy we had with them were beyond any other happiness we had ever known. But

those feelings were fleeting, they came and went. Going back to that anony-mous poem, "Happiness is a thing of here and now," something that comes in moments—not a permanent state of affairs. Where, I wondered, was the more lasting "secret smiling of the heart"?

Linda and I read some things during that time that seemed to back up this don't-expect-more-than-brief-moments-of-joy view of things. The essence was that if you seek happiness, you will never find it—joy and happiness come as the by-products of other worthy goals and pursuits.

We found a quote by Storm Jameson that became important to us: "Happiness? It is an illusion to think that more comfort brings more happi-ness. True happiness comes of the capacity to feel deeply, to enjoy simply, to think freely, to risk life, to be needed."

We had those capacities in our lives; we were finding bits of happiness in our children, in our relationship, in our accomplishments—but we weren't living in joy, and we had begun to think that the more we wanted it, the harder we looked for it, the less likely we were to find it.

We had moved to England by that point, on hiatus from our careers, serv-ing as the directors of several hundred young volunteers doing humanitarian and missionary work and trying to make a difference in people's lives. In the midst of this busy time, we found a quote by Joseph Smith that challenged our recent perspective: "Happiness is the object and design of our existence; and will be the end thereof, if we pursue the path that leads to it."[1]

That quote put us back where we had started, with happiness not as some by-product, but as the goal, the crux, the very purpose of life. It made us wonder if it was our *path* that we should be questioning, not our *goal*. This was a return to our earlier conviction that happiness and joy were pursuable; that happiness was the goal and we needed to find the right path. Joy was the end; we simply had to find the right means to take us there.

What are the means to the end of joy? What are the paths that people are on with the expectation that those paths will lead to the destination of joy?

We pondered those questions for many years in many ways, one of the most unique of which was to go to the self-help section of a giant Barnes & Noble Bookstore on 5th Avenue in Manhattan on the theory that the most common topics or pursuits of self-help are a good indication of the paths

people are pursuing or the means that they hope will lead to the end of happiness.

At the start of the new millennium, wandering through that huge self-help section made it abundantly clear that the three paths, the three things most people were seeking, the three supposed means-to-the-end of happiness that people were writing and reading about, were exactly the topics that dominated the self-help section: how to get more control, how to get more ownership, and how to get more independence. Those bookstore visits became a habit over the years, and though some of the terminology changed to self-fulfillment, stress reduction, and individual freedom, the core pursuits and implied solutions continued to be about getting more control, more independence, and more ownership. The consistent implication and the popular wisdom has been that these are the three things that will lead to joy and happiness.

> What I wanted to do was to examine those connections, to question those assumptions, to see if control, ownership, and independence were really the right paths to happiness.

I realized that what I wanted to do was to examine those connections, to question those assumptions, to see if control, ownership, and independence were really the right paths to happiness. As I began that exploration, some things quickly became clear. Some people were pursuing control, ownership, and independence because they consciously believed that they would lead to happiness. Others were pursuing them simply because it was what everyone else was seeking and it was a way of proving one's self and keeping score.

To make a long story short, I concluded that life, for many of the colleagues I was observing, was like a race where you ran along a track of ever greater control, ownership, and independence, confident that at the finish line of that race was the happiness prize. But the problem was that the farther down

the path people traveled, the clearer it became that the finish line of that particular race was actually *unhappiness*. People were, unwittingly, running in the wrong direction, away from their real goal rather than toward it.

I began to perceive two errors: First, life is not a race, and second, we were all running toward the wrong finish line.

Once I realized that the problem was with the path, I felt compelled to look for a new route, to seek and find opposite-leaning alternatives to control, ownership, and independence, and to form a new happiness paradigm, a new model built around those alternatives.

The seeking of that new paradigm and the search for those three alternatives led Linda and me on an around-the-world odyssey with significant stops at the British Museum, the Holy Land, Carl Jung's Switzerland, the Vatican, the family shrines of Bali, and the ancient island that was once called Serendip.

WARNING . . .

A little warning before we dig deeper: This is not one of those *aha* books where you start nodding your head right away as you grasp why-didn't-I-think-of-that-before truths. In this book, the aha moments will come, but they will come gradually, and they will come only if you stick with me as I suggest to you that some very common attitudes and ambitions you have always thought were good are actually bad, and that some perspectives you have always thought were right are actually wrong.

It won't be easy or natural to accept the ways I am going to ask you to change your mind. In fact, some of what I suggest will seem to go against what your own mother told you, against what your teachers and mentors told you, and against the traditional wisdom that society dumps on you every day. Your instinct may be to resist, to reject, even to resent, because if my premise is true, then on these points at least, your mother was wrong, your teachers were wrong, and the prevailing attitudes you encounter every day are wrong.

No one likes to be wrong, and we like even less to admit that we are wrong. But admitting it is what I have done, and that is what this book will ask you to do—so be warned.

Having said that, let me offer a compensating assurance: If you will hear me out, if you will read this first side of the book with an open mind, you will be able to see the serious errors and problems that exist in three of the perspectives and attitudes we commonly accept in our society today. You will recognize these three thieves of joy and see them for what they are—three deceivers that need to be dismissed, dismantled, and discarded.

Then you will be ready to discover the three alternatives that are presented in the flip side.

A second warning is that I will be highly critical of the assumptions and implied goals of the pervasive self-help industry that surround us today. In a sense, self-help has become the fastest growing religion in this country when measured by book sales or by speaking fees or by what people are talking about when they wax serious or philosophical in their private conversations.

It is not the idea of self-improvement that is bad; it is the three predominant themes or implied objectives that permeate and dominate current self-help books and ideas that work against us.

Finally, one last thing: I'm going to repeat myself occasionally. This is intentional. I will say something in several different ways in my attempt to pry you away from some attitudes that have become part of you. Because the conclusions of the book are so opposite from the prevailing perspectives, it will take a while to adjust, and repetition of some of the fundamental shifting points will make that adjustment gradually grow easier and more natural.

CHAPTER 1

THE THREE
DECEIVERS

The frustration, stress, and imbalance we so often feel are not based as much on what we do or what happens to us as they are on the fact that we are seeking the wrong things—that we have the wrong goals. That is a bold statement, and most people are quite determined to defend the things they are seeking and the goals they have chosen to pursue. Nevertheless, it is a fact that most of us spend a substantial amount of time and mental effort going after three things that actually end up working against us and against our joy and well-being. They are goals that we have been programmed to think are good things, right things, and things that will bring us happiness. Yet it is our entanglement with these three pursuits—of *control, ownership, and independence*—that destroys the balance and the quality of our lives.

THE THREE JOY THIEVES: CONTROL, OWNERSHIP, AND INDEPENDENCE

Before we expand the case for why these are counterproductive goals, ponder for a moment how very, very much we desire each of them and how much effort we put into their pursuit.

Oh, how we long for *control*. We try to control the events of our day by making lists and checking them off. We try to control our children by disciplining and rewarding them. We try to control our destiny by deciding who and where and what we will become. And when things go in a different direction than our plans and our lists and our goals, we feel frustration and stress.

We not only want and wish for control, ownership, and independence, we essentially *worship* these concepts or characteristics. They are our idols. They are the gauges by which we measure success.

Ownership is the American way and the measuring stick of the whole Western world! Life seems to present itself as a giant scoreboard where our success is gauged by what we own. We work longer and harder than any other people in the history of the world because we want more wealth, more possessions—more ownership. And when we compare what we own to what others own (a kind of comparing we seem to find irresistible), the outcome is either envy and jealousy or pride and condescension—both of which lead to unhappiness.

Independence is such a revered concept that over three-quarters of the nations around the world have celebrations surrounding their independence. From America to Azerbaijan, we esteem independence and adopt

the goal personally as well as societally. To need no one, to stand alone, these are the mottos of today. Yet life continually reminds us of how interdependent and dependent we are, and how much we need other people in our lives. We struggle for autonomy, and it can make us feel lonely and isolated.

We not only want and wish for control, ownership, and independence, we essentially *worship* these concepts or characteristics. They are our idols. They are the gauges by which we measure success. They are what our podcasts and our social media and our casual conversations are about. They are the assumed and accepted objectives that cause us to change careers or to get a second job or to move to a new place. They motivate us to avoid having more children, to go further into debt, and to buy better planners and apps and time-management tools. They prompt us to try to manipulate the people and things around us, to accumulate more, and to get through things on our own rather than ask for help.

QUESTIONING THE THREE THIEVES

These thieves not only take joy from us but also deceive us. They are called herein the *three deceivers* because we've been tricked into assuming we want them, into assuming they are good for us. They have grown into obsessions. They are called the *three joy thieves* because that is exactly what they do.

There are two big problems with the concepts of control, ownership, and independence. One is that they cause stress, frustration, and unhappiness. The other is that they represent false values and are, in fact, false and impossible concepts. They are actually illusions. They don't really exist.

Think about it: *What do you really control?* You are one tiny individual in a world full of forces and circumstances that operate completely apart from your will. *What do you really own?* With the one possible exception of your agency or power of choice, you own nothing. You are a *user* of things that pass through your hands. Finally, *from what are you really independent?* You are interdependent with so many other people, especially those you love, and completely dependent on God, Nature, or whatever higher power you perceive for the very air you breathe and the light that lets you live.

Think about the folly of trying to control everything. Life is essentially unpredictable. It happens; little of it is within our control. The measure of our success and happiness lies not in manipulating what happens, but in how we handle and respond to what happens. Constantly trying to control what can't be controlled is a recipe for irritation and stress. Picture yourself at the end of a day when things didn't happen just like you had planned them (pretty much every day) and ask yourself if you enjoyed the surprises or resented them, because that response is really the only thing you can control.

Ponder the fallacy of our obsession with ownership. What do we really own? We may obtain deeds and titles and bank accounts, but they pass through us as we pass through life—so does anything really belong to us? And doesn't the illusion of ownership cause jealousy and envy and condescension and lots of other emotions that connect to *un*happiness? Look at the ways jealousy divides people throughout the world. Picture yourself running around trying to take care of all your things and wishing you had more of them. And then notice children playing and enjoying all the things they don't own. All the best things in life are free, and we can't own any of them.

The bottom line is that we can never have much real control, ownership, or independence.

Consider our misplaced desire for independence. We are all interconnected and interdependent in so many ways. We need each other, and it is these needs that make us human, allow us to love, and encourage us to make commitments. Too much emphasis on independence leads to isolation. Picture yourself today and think about how almost everything you have done is dependent on utilities or electricity or machines, or interdependent with people at work or in schools or stores or anywhere in the complex flow of your life. We are anything but independent.

The bottom line is that we can never have much real control, ownership, or independence. And we wouldn't want it even if we could. Too much control would take the adventure and spontaneity out of life. Too much

ownership becomes bondage. And too much independence equals loneliness and isolation.

Regardless of our differing spiritual beliefs, when we really stop to think about it, most of us can see the limits and the falsehoods in the ideas of control, ownership, and independence. As believers in a spiritual reality, as partakers of the insights and truths that come with faith (and polls tell us that 90 percent of Americans believe in some spiritual force[2]), we know, and should be so grateful, that control and ownership lie with a power much greater than ourselves. We are completely dependent on the higher laws of a higher power.

The first time I remember consciously questioning what I was pursuing (and, believe me, I was in HOT pursuit of the three deceivers) was toward the end of undergraduate college. I had just lost the election for student body president, and my girlfriend had broken off our relationship because, as she said, I was "just too self-centered and too obsessed with all [my] big-time goals."

I was dejected on one level, but I remember that the kind of discouraged, humble feeling I was experiencing somehow felt good to me: mellow and deep. Losing that election and that girl seemed to take the pressure off of me and put me in a quieter place where I felt more in touch with my inner self. I remember thinking, for the first time, that maybe there was a better, less aggressive way to approach life and to view what was happening. I had no idea what that better way was, but it was the opening of a little door that made me begin to wonder if the control, ownership, and independence I was so frantically seeking were really what I wanted.

SOME CONCESSIONS

Now, let's back off a bit and make some caveats and concessions before this starts sounding a little extreme. Control, ownership, and independence are very useful *economic* concepts and are also at least partially true and useful

psychologically. It's good to control our checkbooks and our emotions. Ownership and property rights are essential in a democracy and a free economy, and trying to live with relative independence in an economic sense is certainly a virtue.

Also—and we will go deeper on this one in future chapters—control, ownership, and independence can be correctly thought of as a stage in life—a phase that most people have to live through before they can find a higher and more spiritual paradigm in which to exist. Thinking in terms of control, ownership, and independence is the direction we want to go as we leave our childhood, and it is where we want our children to go as we teach them to accept responsibility and to develop self-reliance and self-discipline. Part of maturity is learning to control our emotions, our appetites, and our finances. Part of responsibility is learning to earn and to own and to take care of things, and we also want our children to take ownership of their grades and their goals. And all parents, whether we verbalize it this way or not, have the goal of working ourselves out of a job—helping our kids to be more and more independent and to need us less and less. So, besides being necessary economically, this is a desirable learning phase that everyone should go through.

The illusion of control, ownership, and independence is a useful phase, and, if we understand it properly, it can be a stepping-stone to three higher alternatives.

The problem comes when we stay in that stage too long and it becomes more obsessive and prevents us from realizing that there is something better and something truer. The problem comes when we desire control, ownership, and independence so much that we let the addiction take over our lives so that we never find the time or the insight we need to pull ourselves back and understand that these things are not actually attainable, nor would we want these three deceivers even if they were.

Interestingly then, the illusion of control, ownership, and independence is a useful phase, and, if we understand it properly, it can be a stepping-stone to three higher alternatives.

The breakthrough comes when we realize (see with our real eyes) that we don't actually want the joy thieves. That realization is what frees us up to look for something better. With that in mind, ponder a couple of *"really"* questions:

Would you *really* like to control your life and the lives of those around you, or is that control better left to a higher power? Would you *really* like to own things that actually belong to us all or to something cosmic or spiritual ("your" children, "your" talents, or the various parts of the earth that you "own")? And would you *really* want to be independent and alone rather than interdependent and connected?

The deeper, spiritual purposes and joys of life would be destroyed and frustrated if we really did have control and ownership and independence. How much more conducive to happiness it is to acknowledge our lack of control, ownership, and independence and do our best to learn to cope, get along, and develop under the circumstances and situations life puts us in.

What we need is a clear and correct *alternative* to each of the three false concepts. As we try to stop seeking and being obsessed with control, ownership, and independence, we need true replacement options to turn our attention and desire toward.

And there *are* true alternatives incorporated within a more complete view of life. Turning away from the three deceivers and focusing instead on their more spiritual alternatives is the key to accessing the happiness and joy that surrounds us—all we need to know is where (and how) to look.

Genuine balance in life, and the peace and fulfillment that come with that balance, is an inner thing obtained only by putting our desires in harmony with reality and with the way this world really works.

CHAPTER 2

WHY WE MUST DISPEL THE DECEIVERS BEFORE WE CAN ADOPT THEIR ALTERNATIVES

C hapter one was originally written as a widely circulated article, and it produced quite a response. The concept of control, ownership, and independence as bad things that work against our happiness rather than good things that bring us happiness struck a chord in many people and caused them to think and to worry. In my back-and-forth comments with readers of that article, we explored how the three deceivers work together to create frustration and discouragement; and we began to use the shorthand initialism of "CO&I" to talk about them collectively as a perspective and a paradox that works against our happiness.

Something deep inside each of us seems to recognize them for what they are—counterfeits, robbers of our peace and joy, and separators of us from our truest selves. For the next few chapters, our focus will be on the damage that our subconscious obsessions with CO&I—control, ownership, and independence—are doing to us.

The reason the other half of this book is reversed and turned upside down is that we need to physically separate these three deceivers from their three alternatives. But before those alternatives will be fully meaningful to you, or fully useful, you will have to be completely convinced that control, ownership, and independence can be dangerous and deceitful concepts that lead us in directions we don't really want to go.

At this early point, you may be a long way from being convinced of that— because much of your life has been devoted to the pursuit of these three things, and few of us want to admit that we have been aiming in wrong directions. Even if we quickly recognize CO&I as deceivers, we may need some reinforcement before we find the courage to try to turn our lives away from them.

Recognize also that there are links between the three deceivers; they feed on each other and each of the three fosters and encourages the other two. They are all materialistic instincts that can cause us to isolate ourselves and judge others. They are secular instincts that do not allow for the deeper acceptance and spirituality that could turn us toward authentic happiness.

When we are thoroughly convinced not only that they are the wrong thing to pursue, but that we must fight them and replace them with something better, we will have a better chance to make a full commitment to the alternatives. For so many—in fact to some degree for all of us—control, ownership, and independence have become the conscious and subconscious targets of our lives. In too many cases they have grown into the framework and the parameters of how we think and of what we want to be. And they have a profound effect on the choices we make and the way we live.

As a management consultant early in my life and as a speaker and presenter later, I often asked individual clients or whole audiences to share their goals with me. Early on, as a consultant, I wanted to know people's goals so I could try to help them achieve them. But I

began to notice patterns in their goals that concerned me—and that worried me about my own goals. First, most of the goals were about achievements and few were about relationships. Second, most of the goals were competitive—about winning something that would make someone else lose. Third, virtually all the goals were about control, ownership, or independence, the usual bottom line was that they believed the things they were trying to control, to own, or not to need would make them happier. But these goals, as I observed them in others and in myself, created a framework of materialism and self-focus that often spiraled away from joy. Achieving some ownership led not to satisfaction but to wanting more, and to the desire to win more control, and took time and focus away from relationships and created an isolating facade of independence.

It was thinking about those goals, and their hoped-for connection to joy, that led me to write some of the articles that eventually led to this book. Now when I ask people to share their goals it is not so that I can help them achieve them, but so that I can help them change them into goals that have more to do with relationships, that value people more than things, that are more win-win than win-lose, and that tap into higher yet humbler attitudes.

There is a direct 1:1 opposite alternative for each of the three deceivers—three antithesis attitudes that can be named, adopted, and substituted—and that will produce the opposite results. They will produce peace instead of stress, cooperation instead of competition, teamwork instead of tension.

BEWARE OF WHAT YOU WANT . . .
FOR YOU MAY GET IT!

It's a somewhat frightening thought: *Beware of what you want, for you may get it.* As human beings, our objectives, even the subconscious or unconscious ones, affect everything we do. The most dangerous misperceptions are the subtle ones because they deceive us without our awareness and we

do not sense their danger. The herd mentality influences us all in spite of our abhorrence of it . . . and the herd is charging toward the graven images of control, ownership, and independence. We can be unduly influenced by our environment, our peers, advertising, social media, and cyberspace, all of which surround and impact us daily. We tend to want what other people want or what other people have or what other people tell us we should want.

But deep down, within our spiritual selves, we somehow know what is real and what is lasting, and thus what we should be pursuing and working for. But, especially in our age of devices and screens and instant messaging, the things right in front of our face or in the palm of our hand seem to grab away our attention from the deeper things, and we live our day-to-day lives going after the temporary and the transitory rather than thinking about and working for what really matters.

In our urban society, we are surrounded by others, competing with others, watching social media and ads and websites and blogs featuring people who seem to have everything they want (and everything we want). We can easily find ourselves falling into the pursuit of society's definition of success rather than developing our own. Since everyone in our society seems to want certain things, it is easy to assume, subconsciously, that we want them too. This is an enormously dangerous assumption.

> Perhaps the most important thing we can examine is what we want and why we want it.

Socrates said, "The unexamined life is not worth living." Perhaps the most important thing we can examine is what we want and why we want it. If we don't examine these key concepts, we fall into assumptions that are highly influenced by the media, our peers, social media, and the world.

For example, we assume that we want proactive, check-off-my-list *control* of our everyday lives, and that we would be happier if we had it. We assume that we want to *own* nicer clothes and a newer car and a better smartphone and a bigger house, and that we would be happier if we had those things. We assume that we want to be more *independent* and autonomous and that we would be happier if we were.

What is interesting is that the wanting-to-be-happier part of each assumption is the true and correct part. The best answer to the ultimate question of what we want is *to be happy.* Happiness is our conscious goal, and it is the right goal. The problem comes not with the conscious goal, but with the subconscious, unexamined pursuits of the things we assume will give us happiness—the pursuit of control, ownership, and independence.

The unexamined goal is not worth pursuing.

BEWARE OF WHAT YOU ASSUME

Of course, as mentioned, control, ownership, and independence are desirable on some levels. We should control our budgets, our emotions, our passions, and our diets; we do own our agency and our choices; and certainly, a degree of financial independence can be a good thing.

But we—and the society all around us—carry CO&I so much further than that. The three deceivers get broadly defined as highly desirable and become the yardstick by which we measure ourselves and others. We want to control more and more, and all the situations and people we can't control begin to frustrate us. We want to own more and more, and we become jealous of those who have more and judgmental toward those who have less. We want to be more and more independent, which separates us from other people and from our spirituality. We get caught up with runaway or extreme applications of the deceivers without examining our own assumptions.

Figuring this out is one thing but knowing what to do about it is another.

I had a friend many years ago who figured all of this out but didn't know what to do about it. He became aware that the materialism and commercialism and competition all around him were making him unhappy and he concluded that what he wanted to do was to simply resign from the rat race. He did it by dropping out—trusting his life to fate instead of to goals and plans. He found that drugs helped him to disengage from the aspirations and from the ambitions that he had concluded were making him unhappy. He essentially replaced

the three deceivers with the even greater deception that his life didn't matter and that any kind of goals or sense of purpose were a waste of time. He became a thrill seeker and an addict and lost his family and his home.

Many, like my friend, who have realized that the headlong pursuit of control, ownership, and independence brings unhappiness, have gone in an opposite direction that is just as extreme and just as damaging. They have given up their proactive tendencies and essentially substituted no goals for false goals. And often they have become even more unhappy.

What we must do, instead, is replace false goals with true goals—with objectives that are in harmony with emotional and spiritual realities. We must find the three alternatives and discard and disavow the three deceivers. We must find the true paradigms or attitudes that can rescue our joy from the three joy thieves.

By now, you may have begun to get your own ideas about what the three alternative attitudes might be. But remember this: to be correct, the three alternatives must preserve all of the good aspects of the deceivers (initiative, motivation, discipline, etc.) but eliminate all of the negative aspects (judgment, jealousy, conceit, presumption, envy, covetousness, etc.). I invite you to write down what you think the alternatives are and modify your guesses as you read on.

—

CHAPTER 3

HOW THE DECEIVERS DECEIVE

There are three particular ways we get deceived and carried away into the pursuit of CO&I—three vehicles that can confuse us and that we are particularly susceptible to. These vehicles are appearances, media and social media, and false paradigms.

HOW APPEARANCES DECEIVE

We live in a world where appearances seem to be the main reality. In our effort to look good to others, we get caught up with the questions of how and

where and who and when. We forget to ask ourselves the most important question: *Why*. We ask ourselves: *How* can I make more money and get more independence? *Where* is the most prestigious place to live? *Who* are the people to know and be seen with? And *when* will I finally gain full control of my life? Instead, we should be asking *why* we really want these things and what we may have to sacrifice to get them.

Appearances deceive us because others around us, both the real people and the media people (our real neighbors and our cyber neighbors, our sitcom characters or Facebook friends) always look and act like everything is going great for them. They have a lot of things we want, and they seem to be very happy because of those things. Their lives look a little (or a lot) more in control than our own lives feel.

And they don't seem to have to depend on anyone but themselves. Think about those TV series where the people are all alone surviving in the wilderness—the producers never show us the camera guy, snack table, or rescue people waiting on the sidelines. Think about your friend next door or on Facebook with the great job, designer furniture, and perfect children— you don't see the challenges or heartache, just the nicely pressed outfit and fun vacation photos.

> **Others are putting on appearances to impress us and we are putting on appearances to impress them. We are both succeeding and both deceiving.**

What we don't always realize is that we look much the same to our neighbors. The deceptive mirror works both ways and we unwittingly deceive each other by looking better than we really are. Essentially, others are putting on appearances to impress us and we are putting on appearances to impress them. We are both succeeding and both deceiving.

HOW MEDIA AND
SOCIAL MEDIA DECEIVE

All of this is especially true (exaggeratedly true) in the media and social media we consume. Movies and TV programs try to show regular life, but too often, by the end of its run time, problems are solved, relationships resolved, and the slate is clean. In real life, of course, it is never that easy.

There are two parts to the media deception. One part is the media itself—the programs and reality shows and blogs and tweets—and the unrealistic, materialistic, and self-centered view of life they often give us. The second part to the deception is the advertising.

A good friend of mine, the CEO of a giant New York advertising agency (and an unusually candid person, particularly for his industry) told me his personal definition of advertising: "The fine art of making people think they need what they really only want." He also told me that the average American sees (or hears) over five thousand advertising impressions each day. Forbes *echoes these numbers with their estimation of exposure at four thousand to ten thousand impressions a day.[3] Little wonder we think we need more stuff, newer stuff, better stuff.*

The entertainment part of media is just as big a deceiver as the advertising part. Doesn't everyone you see in movies or on TV seem to have more than you do and to have obtained it more easily and to have more control of their stuff and their bigger, better lives? It's all make-believe and illusions, but it seems pretty real—especially with as much TV, movies, and other entertainment as we consume on our large and small screens. Like our ancestors before us, we look through our rectangular, glass windows and observe and envy our neighbors. But unlike our ancestors, we turn those glass windows on and off with a switch.

And if media in general deceives, then social media doubles down and raises the bar of deception. Now it's not only actors and celebrities who look better than they really are, it's our Facebook friends and those we follow on

Instagram—it's the bloggers and the tweeters—who often seem to have more control, ownership, and independence than we do, and they beckon us to follow. This is not real life because they only show us what they want us to see.

It is hard in this connected, media-dominated world, to think for ourselves—to ask more often—*why*. Why do I want what I want? Why do I think I should have to control everything? Why do I want to have more, or at least as much as someone else? Why do I feel the need to be independent of everyone else? If we ask the deep *why* questions, we begin to realize that the honest answers have to do with envy and want and greed rather than with need, and that our assumption about control, ownership, and independence being directly connected and necessary to our happiness is a lie.

Focus on that last statement for a minute: *the connections of control, ownership, and independence to happiness are assumptions and lies.* The media and the internet lead us to the unexamined assumption that owning more and better things will make us happier, that controlling more of our lives and being more independent and less needful of others will give us more happiness.

With some pondering, we know that those implied and assumed connections are false, and that the real connections to happiness lie more with commitment, relationships, interdependence, sharing, delayed gratification, appreciation, service, and faith.

Still, our tendency is to do what others are doing and pursue what others are pursuing.

I was at the Harvard Business School during a very interesting and transitional couple of years. During my first year there, everyone seemed to fit a standard style and protocol. We all went to class in three-piece suits and carried attaché cases and were conservatively groomed. Anti–Vietnam War protests were breaking out at the college across the Charles River, but seemed to have little effect on business-as-usual at the business school.

Summer came, the first year ended, and we all went off on internships. When we returned, everything had changed. The delayed

reaction of unrest finally made it across the river and many business school students became active in political protest and anti-war demonstrations. Hair got long, no one wore a suit or tie, backpacks and cut-offs and jeans and sweatshirts became the order of the day. Debates and sharp differences of opinion were everywhere. Conversations from the previous year about how much money we could make and how long it would take to become a CEO shifted to broader and more serious philosophical discussions about what really mattered and what was right. We were all getting better at asking the question why. Professors had to be sharper and more on their guard because students were disagreeing with them on fundamental things like profit motive and environmental responsibility. For me, the whole environment became more stimulating and interesting—with more chance of new, more unique outlooks, and fresh, more-examined paradigms.

Unfortunately, as the year wore on, most students returned to the focus and mentality of who could make the most money and land the best first job.

HOW FALSE PARADIGMS DECEIVE

A *paradigm* is a viewpoint or inner framework for what we think is reality. It's a word that will become much more important in the other side of this book. The media and the web and all their appearances often lead us to *false* paradigms, to a collection of unrealistic and incorrect views of reality, assumed connections, and wrong worldviews. And the problem is that the false paradigms themselves become the biggest deceivers of all. Because once our view or perspective of something is accepted, even subconsciously, it becomes a filter through which we observe and interpret everything else.

False paradigms don't become true when we accept them, but they do become *highly influential* on our lives, our behavior, our priorities, and our

thoughts. Once I accept the paradigm that I would be happier if I owned more stuff and better stuff, my actions and my whole thought process begins to be governed by the pursuit of more and better stuff. Once I accept the paradigm that cool people are independent and in control, I start criticizing myself for needing and being dependent on others or for not being able to control my life well enough to get everything checked off my list every day. This type of thinking pulls us into the CO&I trap.

> # If you think the world is flat, you are going to make some bad navigation decisions and become increasingly frustrated.

If you think the world is flat, you are going to make some bad navigation decisions and become increasingly frustrated. If you think happiness depends on control, ownership, and independence, you are going to make some bad prioritizing decisions and become increasingly frustrated. Once you correct your paradigm to a round world you will get back on your course or nautical destination. Once you shift your paradigm from the three joy thieves to the three alternatives, you will get back on course to your destination of a happy life.

THE SUBTLETY OF THE DECEPTION

There are some habits or thoughtless patterns we fall into which allow the three deceivers to take hold of us. These are subtle, gradual things. Like all addictions, they grow and take over a little bit at a time. To understand this sinister subtlety, we need to probe three "how"s:

1. How do we get caught up in the race without really thinking about the destination?
2. How do the mirrors and windows of our lives get distorted?

3. How does seeking the wrong things keep us from finding the right things?

HOW WE GET CAUGHT UP IN THE RACE

WITHOUT REALLY THINKING ABOUT

THE DESTINATION

"The Joneses have one, so we should have one." "We have to have the second income so we can have a bigger home." "If we want our kids to get into the right college, we have to be able to pay for the right private school now." "I need a better computer/tablet/smartphone and more effective planning so I can get more control of my life." "Joe has so much more independence than I do. He goes where he wants when he wants." "I need more online friends and followers to validate me." "I'm too dependent on other people and have too many people who are dependent on me."

Getting there faster, doing more, controlling more, having more, and constantly comparing ourselves with those around us has become a way of life for most people. When did life become such a contest, such a race? We ought to remember what Thoreau said, "If a man fails to keep pace with his companions, perhaps it is because he hears a different drummer. Let him move to the beat he hears, no matter how measured or far away." And we ought to remember what e. e. cummings said: "more, more, more, more, my hell, what are we all becoming, morticians?"

Part of the problem is that we live so close to each other both in reality and in virtual reality that comparing is easy. Another part of the problem is that we are surrounded by media that is always making comparisons for us and setting up false "ideals" that we are all expected to desire. We slip subtly into the race for CO&I, running along with everyone else, running faster and faster, and seeing less and less along the way. Is it really a race we want to be in? And are the "rewards" of control, ownership, and independence really the prizes we want to win? Or do we want to consciously drop out of that race and seek our happiness in other, very different places?

HOW OUR MIRRORS AND WINDOWS
BECOME DISTORTED

There was an amusement park near our house where I grew up, and one vivid boyhood memory I have is standing with my brother in front of the wavy glass mirrors in the fun house laughing riotously at our big heads or short legs in those comical reflections. Our grandkids now have apps that do the same kind of silly face-changing.

The old carnival mirrors made us laugh because they distorted everything. Today's mirrors of fashion and of self-image, which try to reflect what the world seems to want us to be, can be equally distorting.

Even worse than old wavy glass or circus mirrors is when our *windows* start turning into *mirrors* and we lose our ability to see others and their needs. If our windows become coated with the silver of selfishness and absorbing self-awareness, we begin to see only the surface and not through the glass. We see our own reflection, and we see others only in terms of how they can help us or affect our image or fit into our plans. We use the mirrors only as the basis for competition and comparison concerning what we have more of or less of. The deceivers are all about ourselves, all about mirrors.

> If our windows become coated with the silver of selfishness and absorbing self-awareness, we begin to see only the surface and not through the glass.

Anaïs Nin said "We do not see the world as it is, we see it as we are." Or, we see the world as we wish it were or as we wish we were. We think we want more control, more ownership, and more independence, and we fit everything into that model—including other people.

Happiness comes from seeing the world around us, and the people in it, as they really are—*seeing* through windows instead of *looking* at mirrors, being

aware of the needs and feelings of others and serving them when we can. It comes from accepting people as they are and not comparing ourselves to them. It comes from having true perspective about the things that really matter.

HOW SEEKING THE WRONG THINGS KEEPS US
FROM FINDING THE RIGHT THINGS

At times when we have clear perspective and are tuned in to spiritual truth we all know what really matters. We know that our relationships, our families, our health, our character, and our growth as human beings and as interconnected humanity are the things that count. We even know, when our spiritual discernment is clear, that we control very little and that something much larger than ourselves controls all—that ownership is an illusion and independence is not reality. We see that interdependence with each other and dependence on a higher power is both the way it is and the way it should be.

If you've flown over or hiked across the tops of large mountain ranges and seen how they just go on and on, you see your own smallness in the scheme of this earth. You know you are not big or important by any stretch of the imagination. The problem is that these moments of clarity don't come often enough because we don't ask the questions or do the things that generate them.

We live in a world of clamor and activity. On all sides we are confronted with penetrating impressions from media, peers, and society that all tell us we need to control more, own more, be more independent and self-sufficient, and that we must compete and compare on the basis of these false ideals.

The stereotypes of the world not only lead us to false and deceiving objectives; they block our vision and our perception of the real goals. They take our attention away from enjoying all the simple gifts we are given, away from noticing and helping those in need, away from developing our faith and character.

CHAPTER 4

———

A BRIEF HISTORY OF CONTROL, OWNERSHIP, AND INDEPENDENCE

The paradigm of CO&I and the concepts and pursuits of control, ownership, and independence are very difficult to let go of even when we know there are superior (and more spiritual) alternatives. So, it is important, before we flip over to the three rescuers of joy, to go deeper into the problematic nature and powerful destructiveness of the three joy thieves.

In thinking about how to get away from a deceptive concept, it is helpful to know its evolution so that we can see it with perspective and clarity and causality. To do that, it is necessary to take a somewhat historical look of each of the three deceivers and their subtle infiltration into our societal norms.

HOW WE GOT SO CAUGHT
UP WITH CONTROL

The history of the quest for control is essentially the history of the world. On the macro level, wars are fought, boundaries drawn, and laws written in pursuit of control. On the micro, we try to control everything from the temperature of our rooms to the behavior of our kids. Human beings seem hardwired with the desire to control the things around them. We want to act rather than be acted upon. This internal programming has probably saved our lives individually and collectively and it motivates a lot of goals and plans and actions, but it so often goes much too far.

In recent history, this instinct to control has been institutionalized by the whole industry of time management and goal-setting and by the notion that control is what can bring us happiness. The good notion of setting goals and making plans and controlling oneself gets expanded into the false idea that we should be able to control and manage everything (and everyone) around us. Yet in reality, we have control of a tiny island of things around which swirls in a huge sea of uncontrollability and unpredictability. Our challenge is not to control the ocean, but to see its beauty and appreciate and learn how best to ride on its waves and currents.

In reality, we have control of a tiny island of things around which swirls in a huge sea of uncontrollability and unpredictability.

In the control mode, surprises annoy or irritate us because they may prevent our day from going exactly as we had planned. Our friends annoy us because they don't do things the way we would. Our children annoy us because they don't seem to want to do exactly what we want them to or be interested in just what we think should interest them. And days when we don't get everything checked off of our list get chalked up as failures because we have defined success as control.

Striving to control our emotions, our appetites, and our habits is good and praiseworthy. However, we must strive with equal diligence to acknowledge that we are fragile and vulnerable and need help in everything we do, even in our most personal improvement goals. When our instinct and desire to control go unchecked, we edge toward the definition of a control freak and the result is the irritation of others and the frustration of ourselves.

Bottom line: there must be a better and more accurate attitude than control.

HOW WE GOT SO CAUGHT UP WITH OWNERSHIP

The right to own property is a key underpinning of a democracy and a free-enterprise system. This right had to be fought for and won in order to free people from tyrants and monarchy. The American Revolution is only one example of the endless struggle for autonomy and free enterprise.

In an economic sense, ownership is a prerequisite for responsibility. People aren't as likely to take good care of things unless they own them. Generally, we take better care of our own cars than rental cars, and a vacation rental is more likely to be abused than your own home. But, like control, ownership becomes deceptive and destructive when it is taken too far. When an ownership mentality takes over our thinking, we forget that ownership is temporary. We are just using things which pass through our hands—things which come from or are part of the earth, things we may have a deed for, but which ultimately belong to God or to humanity.

If you think of the notion of ownership as the trunk of a tree, what are the branches that grow? Branches of envy and jealousy sprout as we are in contact with those who have more things or better things than we do. Branches of condescension or superiority shoot up as we see those who have less. Branches of greed and covetousness begin to grow as we think about all that we wish we had. Branches of pride germinate as we think about what we have or about having more of it than someone else.

Bottom line: there must be a better perspective, a better paradigm than ownership.

We were living in suburban Northern Virginia just outside Washington, DC, as I started a new political consulting firm; during the same time, my gradual suspicion of control, ownership, and independence was starting to grow.

The community church we attended had a program of home visits where people kept track of each other by having regular contact with two or three other families from the congregation to see how they were doing and whether they had any needs that the church might help with. The two families I visited couldn't have been more different from each other. One was the family of a hard-driving entrepreneur who was one of the most aggressive and self-driven people I have ever met. The other was the family of a skilled carpenter and his stay-at-home wife and their six kids. Initially I had a lot of attraction to and admiration of the guy in the first family (let's call him Jim) and a lot of pity for the second (George).

Jim had a Ferrari. He lived in a modern mansion with a separate pool house and a tennis court. He talked fast and had deals going everywhere. Jim had a lot of control, ownership, and independence. George lived in a tiny house with one bathroom, his hands were always stained, and the obtaining of control, ownership, and independence did not seem to be his main concern.

My feelings about these two families shifted over time. Jim's relationships were in shambles, his marriage on the rocks, and his kids entitled and rebellious. I felt palpable tension in that big glass house every time I was there. I began to dread my visits. Going to see George and his family, on the other hand, was always a kind of peaceful pleasure. They were not wealthy, but they were close. They smiled a lot and seemed grateful for what they had. Was this what happiness looks like? I wondered.

For me, the contrasts between these two families represented another little milestone in my gradual journey away from the joy thieves.

HOW WE GOT SO CAUGHT UP
WITH INDEPENDENCE

How can one speak or write against independence in a land founded on it and emancipated by a document called the Declaration of Independence? Of course, independence is a desirable political condition, and of course personal independence is an asset in the sense of thinking for oneself and taking care of oneself.

But like the other deceivers, it gets dangerous and damaging when it is carried too far—especially when it is carried into our spiritual lives and our relationships. We have become a world that worships independence and equates strength with not needing other people. It is easy to forget, in this mode, how interdependent we all are and how it is our collective intelligence that has allowed us to progress so far as humans.

To need and to be needed is what keeps us human, humble, and honorable.

As Matt Ridley states at the beginning of his book *The Rational Optimist*, "At some point, human intelligence became collective and cumulative in a way that happened to no other animal."[4] He explains that he has, on his desk, two similar sized, man-made objects—one is a Stone Age hand ax and the other is a computer mouse. One was made by one person, the other by thousands of different people, each specialized in one thing but working in tandem to create and produce technology. This collective intelligence and interdependence is what allows the vast progress that independence could never generate.

To need and to be needed is what keeps us human, humble, and honorable.

Perhaps the most dangerous independence construct of all is that it makes it too easy to forget our complete and entire dependence on a higher power that gave us life and now gives us every breath we breathe.

The real problem with Independence is in the *I*. Independence, at the lengths we often try to carry it, is the attitude of I. It's about me and about what I can do on my own. Real life put in proper perspective is always about

we, about us, about our interdependence. It's about how all of us are brothers and sisters and all equally and totally dependent. The old, positive can-do attitude is a great place to start, but a better (and higher) place is a positive can't do attitude that essentially says "by myself, I am nothing and can't do much of anything, but with the help of friends and family, and most of all with guidance and spiritual assistance, I can do things of true meaning."

Bottom line: there must be a better perspective, a better paradigm, than independence.

CHAPTER 5

———

THE UNHAPPINESS FORMULA, ITS PROGRESSION, AND ITS CATALYST

Happiness comes in many forms—but can be divided into two primary types: unhappiness brought upon us by other people and by situations beyond our control, and unhappiness that we bring upon ourselves.

Sickness, injury, loss of a loved one, abuse, and other forms of circumstantial adversity are usually of the first kind. And despite the pain and grief that they bring, they can sometimes be accompanied by silver linings and eventual blessings. As Shakespeare said: "Sweet are the uses of adversity, which, like the toad, ugly and venomous, wears yet a precious jewel in its head. And so our lives, free from public haunt, find tongues in trees, sermons in stone, books in the running brooks, and good in everything."

Within the second category—self-inflicted unhappiness, the excessive, obsessive pursuit of CO&I can begin to take over our lives, and we find ourselves caught in an equation that always equals unhappiness. Yet if we come to understand the fallacies and the limits of the deceivers, we can hold them at bay and learn from them even as we seek deeper truth and a higher paradigm. We might modify Shakespeare's verse to express the pain and gain of this second kind of unhappiness: Sweet are the uses of control, ownership, and independence if we can expose their flaws and limits even as we learn their lessons, we can be pointed toward something better. And then our lives, free from its further pursuit, find the present joy of tongues in trees and books in the running brooks.

THE UNHAPPINESS EQUATION

Imagine that you were tasked with the dark job of creating a formula or an equation for unhappiness. $X + Y + Z = U$ (Unhappiness). What would X, Y, and Z be?

If you were analytical about it, you might start by looking for the things that contribute most obviously and predictably to unhappiness—stress, anxiety, worry, feelings of inadequacy, irritation, business and overwork, loneliness, toxic relationships, isolation.

But adding all those things up creates too long a formula—you are looking for a more basic equation, so you begin looking for the source or cause of all of these forms of unhappiness. What makes us susceptible to them? What lets them into our lives? What allows them to grab us?

The formula has to be something within us, some mental back door that lets unhappiness in and that weakens our natural state of joy. This needs to be a fundamental formula—the most basic elements which work in a simple equation. Three factors, three parts of us that let in and stir up and magnify all the fears, feelings, fatigues, and frustrations that compose unhappiness.

The most basic things we possess are our desires and attitudes, and if some of these encompass or are conducive to all those negative feelings, then we are getting close to the simple formula for unhappiness.

What pursuit is more conducive to frustration and irritation than trying to *control* everything and everyone and not realizing that most things and people can't and shouldn't be controlled? What goal is more likely to lead to anxiety and feelings of inadequacy than *ownership* and the constant inclination to compare and compete on everything? And what approach links more closely to loneliness and isolation than insisting that you don't need others and are completely *independent*?

Simple equation: C + O + I = U. Attitudes of control, ownership, and independence equal unhappiness. Pursuing these opens the way to the irritation, inadequacy, and isolation that are the building blocks of unhappiness and the blockers of joy.

THE UNHAPPINESS PROGRESSION

The frightening thing about our unhappiness formula is that it is not static. It doesn't just produce a little unhappiness and then stop. It is dynamic—it grows and progresses and produces more and more unhappiness as long as we let it operate in our lives.

Progression is often a positive concept. We progress in our development of skills or in our mastery of a subject. We progress from grace to grace or from gift to gift.

But there also negative progressions, slippery slopes where our slide gets faster and faster and harder and harder to stop, downward spirals where we lose control and plummet toward darkness. In today's world, there are two dark progressions that should scare us most, two quicksand dangers that should deeply concern us all. One is the way wants can progress into obsessions, which can then quickly turn into addictions.

Wants ⋯⟩ *Obsessions* ⋯⟩ *Addictions*

The other is similar, but more complicated, because it can be a good or a bad progression. It is the progression of acceptance to belief and then of

belief to worship. The danger of this progression is that it can happen with false-hoods and carefully crafted lies as well as with truth.

> *Acceptance* ····> *Belief* ····> *Worship or Allegiance*

An example of the first negative progression is someone who wants social acceptance or to be free of some kind of stress or pain so badly that he or she becomes obsessed with comparing body types against the supposed ideal and becomes addicted to anorexic or bulimic behavior.

With the second kind of progression, on the good side, someone *accepts* the love of piano music and the notion that one could learn to play, progresses to competence, and comes to love and admire and share music. Or someone accepts the idea of spirituality and progresses to belief and faith and is thus driven to worship and service. On the bad side, someone accepts a false idea about materialism or power or release from responsibility and soon begins to believe in things that are untrue and then to worship wealth or fame or imagined freedom.

As big a concern as these progressions are on things like substance abuse or pornography or materialism, we should be most concerned and most determined to avoid negative progressions that act on our *attitudes*.

I remember applying for a position many years ago where the preinterview questionnaire posed the question, "Do you have any addictions?" I ticked the "no" box. I had always been an athlete and the combination of warnings and encouragements from coaches and from my parents had kept me free from substance abuse. So it was easy to check "no." It was about that time, however, that I had begun to be concerned about the obsessive directions in which my life seemed to be leading me. I had a lot and I wanted more. I was traveling too much with work, sleeping and exercising too little, out of touch with Linda and our kids. But bigger prizes and possessions were more and more within reach and I had my pedal to the metal. The good news—though I didn't recognize it as such at the time—was that I had begun to worry that I was addicted to CO&I. This worry or awareness forced me to examine my attitudes.

Control, ownership, and independence have become our mental and emotional obsessions.

The problem with obsessions, of course, is that they lead to addictions. Instead of letting the negative progression continue, we must find ways to reverse it—to go backward to our *wants* instead of forward toward *addictions*. We must attack this progression at its beginning.

We can begin this approach by questioning our wants and beliefs, by asking ourselves why we want or believe certain things, by asking ourselves if they are the right things to pursue. We can examine and operate on our wants before they balloon into obsessions and then mutate into addictions that eclipse our healthy wants and needs. We can consider our acceptance of ideas and trends before adding them to our belief systems and we can check what we desire or what we allow to consume our energy. We must ask ourselves if we would rather have our own control or spiritual guidance, if we want selfish ownership or selfless sharing, and if we want the loneliness of independence or the connectedness of interdependence.

> We can consider our acceptance of ideas and trends before adding them to our belief systems and we can check what we desire or what we allow to consume our energy.

THE UNHAPPINESS CATALYST

But now a provocative question: Is the unhappiness of the joy thieves always something we bring upon ourselves, or could there also be an external aspect to this unhappiness formula and this dangerous progression? Could there be some force, some being, some external influence that wants us to be unhappy and that nudges us away from our natural state of joy?

Virtually everything in life has its light side and its dark side. Just as there are literal forces of good, there are literal forces of evil. Good exists. Evil exists. And both love company. Good tries to persuade us to do good; evil tries to persuade us to do evil.

You will have to decide for yourself whether you believe in an ultimate being of good and an ultimate being of evil, but whether these are personal embodiments or simply existing forces in our world, they do exist.

As mentioned earlier, control, ownership, and independence are useful economic and political concepts that foster free enterprise, discipline, and certain types and levels of responsibility. Yet they each become deceivers when carried into emotional and spiritual realms or when our thinking and our goals are based on their paradigm. Evil uses the popularity and self-centered appeal of the deceivers to pull us down and away from higher principles. It popularizes and glorifies them to the point that they become our measurements of success (for ourselves and for others) and to the point where they become first our obsessions and then our addictions—first our ideals and then our idols. Once we are wanting and worshipping them enough, we become dulled down and steered off the path to happiness in various ways with sundry strategies. One of these strategies of evil is *overload*.

THE STRATEGY OF OVERLOAD

Much has been written about the value and benefits of adversity. None of us wish for it, but most of us have learned that it will always come, in small ways and big, and that if we survive it well, we can emerge a better, stronger person.

The trouble is that the darker side has learned the same thing. Hardships and other kinds of personal adversity produce pain and suffering for a while. However, people who suffer adversity often arise stronger and more stalwart for it, and thus move in opposite directions (discipline, devotion, empathy, service, and happiness) from where the evil sends them. Consequently, like any fierce competitor, evil changes its strategy.

The new approaches include comfort and ease, acute materialism, satisfaction and idleness. However, one of its best new approaches could be called overload. Evil knows that in a world so complex, so demanding, so overflowing with options and alternatives—if there is an overlay of compulsive comparing and competitive envy and pride—we can be completely distracted from introspective, contemplative thought and reflection. We will be too distracted to seek good. If our minds can be kept on what we want, they will never stray to what good wants. If we are exhausted every day from our pursuit of the world, we will have little energy left to see the needs of others or to examine where we are headed. If we are kept occupied with our obsessions for control, ownership, and independence, we will have neither the time nor the desire to think about guidance or service or our dependence on the spiritual and our interdependence with others.

The solution, and our defense against overload and against the unhappiness catalyst, can center on learning to more frequently ask ourselves the question: WHY?

Answers that relate to the true good of our family and the welfare of others and community are good answers.

We are prone to spend our mental energy asking (and answering) the questions of what (what we own, what we want, what is cool, what will make us look good), where (where we want to live, where we want to travel), who (who are the best contacts, who do we want to be seen with), when (when do we want our promotion or our independence) and how (how do we get more control, how do we win the many games we are playing). These are mostly control, ownership, and independence questions and they can be dangerous when they are not preceded by what should be the first question: Why. It is the *why* questions that cause us to ponder, prioritize, and seek for guidance and inspiration and insight. Why do we want what we want? Why do we do what we do? Why is a powerful question because it makes us dig deep and be honest with ourselves, and when we are honest, we know whether the answers are good or bad. Answers that relate only to appearances, competing and winning, and comfort and ease are not

good answers. Answers that relate to the true good of our family and the welfare of others and community are good answers.

Why is also a good question because answering it honestly can often help us to simplify our lives and to break free of the overload. When we don't have a good answer for why we do something, we may be able to stop doing it—to eliminate one more complexity from our lives, and to thus put greater focus and greater priority on things that really matter.

A second part of the solution is to think of our lives as a series of mirrors and windows. Mirrors reflect ourselves and windows reveal others. We all need some of each. We need to try to see ourselves, not through the selfish, competitive, and covetous mirrors of the world, but through accurate mirrors of how we are measuring up to our potential, to our best potential destinies. It is so important to balance the mirrors with windows—to try to be transparent as much as we can, focusing on others rather than our own reflections. What does my child need? What does my spouse need? What does my friend need? What does this stranger need?

My wife, Linda, was a shy and insecure (somewhat hard to imagine now) adolescent who had a very wise mother. The eighth-grade dance was coming up; it was required attendance and Linda's most dreaded event. She tried to get out of it by feigning sickness, but her mom saw through it and knew what the real problem was. She gave her daughter a challenge: "Linda," she said, "I want you to go to that dance with one thing on your mind—to find someone who looks even more uncomfortable and miserable than you. Then I want you to go talk to that person and find out all you can about her." Linda did that and it worked—it took her mind off of herself and she met Shirley, who became her good friend and her companion in the battle to get through awkward adolescence. Linda describes it as her first windows experience.

Windows and why questions make us think and can help us simplify and thus to begin to overcome the incredibly widespread problem of overload.

CHAPTER 6

———

CHANGING OUR
DEFINITION OF
SUCCESS

ll| make myself rich by making my wants few." This sentiment has been
expressed by Thoreau and many others. It contains a deep truth that
takes many of us a long time to recognize. The truth is that if we want
the right things, we will find that we already have them—and that they are all
we need.

Essentially, there are two ways to pursue happiness in this world. One is to
adopt the measurements of the society around us and exhaust ourselves competing with everyone else to own more, to control more, and to need others
less. These "measures of success" that we so often judge and are judged by,
seem to be held up in front of us everywhere we look as the standard that will
make us happy—as the things that everyone should want and want and want.

An alternative way to pursue happiness is to change the definition of what
success is. If we consciously reject the measurements of control, ownership,

and independence by reminding ourselves that while they may be useful economic concepts, they are spiritual deceptions, and if we redefine success as the receiving of blessings, guidance, and the gifts of relationships, we will realize that we already have all that we need to be happy.

> *One of our sons has a story that is worth a thousand words or a thousand pictures. In the midst of a successful career as a builder of ten-million-dollar homes in Las Vegas, he and his wife began to ask the question why. Why do people need twenty thousand feet of living space? Why do we feel that life is a competition? Why don't we value simplicity more? Why don't we put more effort into relationships and less into achievements? The questions led to huge lifestyle changes, and they now live simply with their five children on an island in a tiny but beautiful home on a budget of less than one thousand dollars a month. They consume little electricity, grow or trade for most of their food, and drive cars that operate on vegetable oil. Their kids babysit and mow lawns and buy their own stuff. The family is the perfect ex-ample of making themselves rich by making their wants few.*

With true, soulful goals replacing the false and carnal goals of the world, many useful variations of "I make myself rich by making my wants few" become possible:

"I make myself happy by changing my definition of success."

"I make myself rich by wanting only the simple gifts of beauty and relationships."

"I make myself joyful by recognizing and appreciating what blessings I already have."

One of the best interpretations of the well-known Bible saying "Be in the world but not of the world" is that it is possible to live in modern, secular so-ciety, and indeed to appreciate it for all it offers, yet not to become obsessed with the same pursuits that those around us covet and seek.

Trying to own more than our neighbors, to control everyone and every-thing around us, and to be independent of other people are misplaced goals. They lead to frustration and unhappiness. And they are the worst definitions of success.

John Robbins, who walked away from the Baskin Robbins fortune in pursuit of a simpler life, put it this way: "When we say someone is a 'success,' what do we mean? Do we mean that she or he is an emotionally balanced, loving human being? Do we mean that this person is creative and artistic and adds beauty to the world? Not usually. Instead, most of us reserve the word 'success' for people who have made a lot of money. This is how we impoverish ourselves."[5]

THE DECEPTIVE MODELS
OF THE WORLD

Have you noticed how everything in our world seems to be measured, evaluated, and valued in economic terms? From the personal ways in which we judge people (wealth, appearance, success) to the way we try to understand the broader world (GNP, productivity, recession), we base our opinions on parts of a giant and pervasive economic model.

Another worldly model is the competitive model where there is always a winner and a loser, one who controls and one who is controlled. It is a power paradigm where our judgments and evaluations are based on who has more or less power.

And a final cultural icon of modern measurement is something that could be called the individual options model. We judge everything by whether or not it limits our full range of opportunities or gets in the way of our "freedom" to do whatever we want.

What is incomplete about these models?

Simply that they ignore the spirit, they ignore the soul, they ignore the necessity of sacrifice and commitment, and they largely ignore family and friendships. They are materialistic, temporary models that fail to take into account long-term perspectives, our interdependence, our need to love and to be loved, or our need to believe in something higher than ourselves and to hope for magic and meaning beyond what our eyes can see.

The three models fit, one to one, with the three deceivers. The economic model matches up with the ownership deception. The competitive model coincides with the deception of control. And the individual options model overlays the independence deception.

THINK OF CONTROL, OWNERSHIP, AND INDEPENDENCE AS A STAGE OF LIFE, BUT DON'T LINGER

Let's once again step back a bit and give control, ownership, and independence a little credit and even acknowledge that it may constitute a useful phase or stage of life that most of us have to go through before we can go beyond.

> Is it possible that we might want to help our children grow into control, ownership, and independence at the same time that we ourselves are trying to grow out of it?

As parents, we certainly try to teach control, ownership, and independence to our children. We want our kids to be able to control their tempers, their appetites, and the use of their time. We want them to take responsibility or ownership of their toys, their clothes, their school work, and even their friendships. And we want them to gradually grow more independent of us—more self-sufficient and more self-motivated.

So, is it possible that we might want to help our children grow into control, ownership, and independence at the same time that we ourselves are trying to grow out of it?

Of course, this is possible—and ultimately, it is the best way to think about control, ownership, and independence—as a stage of life that can teach us

a lot as we pass through it—as a grade in school in which we do our best before being promoted to the next level. Think of it as the elementary school of life that we don't want to carry over into the university of our adult life.

There is something appropriate and appealing about a ten-year-old or a fifteen-year-old who is showing self-control, accepting responsible ownership for her things, and not needing her parents in everything she does and every choice she makes. But an adult who clings too obsessively to the same paradigm grows far less appealing if he becomes rigid or dominant or manipulative in his control, greedy and prideful and competitive in his ownership, or unreceptive to others and invulnerable in his independence.

The key is to develop the self-discipline and self-reliance that can stem from CO&I and carry these qualities into our adulthood as we become our best selves and create the structure of our lives. We then need to perceive the next step which involves moving above the paradoxes of these incomplete attitudes and approaches and finding a higher, truer paradigm.

Richard Rohr, in his book *Falling Upward*, puts it this way, "There are at least two major tasks to human life. The first task is to build a strong 'container' or identity; the second is to find the contents that the container was meant to hold."[6]

Control, ownership, and independence are useful building blocks in the construction of our container, but it is important to recognize when we are finished building it and to refocus on what goes inside—seeking the deeper content of what our lives will hold.

After all, life is best thought as a progression, and we are better off with our eyes and our hearts on the more spiritual and more perceptive stage of life that we are evolving into—not looking back over our shoulder and longing to be young again. Filling our containers is ultimately a happier job than building them.

This book is about finding and moving into a new, second stage of life and making that move as early as we can. So, as we wrap up this side of the book, think of control, ownership, and independence as a phase we go through, learning its valuable lessons, and then moving out and up into the higher perspective of the three alternatives.

CHAPTER 7

—

FROM PARADOX TO PARADIGM

When I started writing this book, I had four objectives:

1. *Expose* the three deceivers of control, ownership, and independence and show the ways that they can rob us of
   both our happiness and our full potential in life.
2. *Create* a framework in which the three alternatives could
   be clearly presented and effectively implemented in our
   thoughts and our lives.
3. *Reveal* the three alternatives and illustrate how they preserve the truths and benefits of the three deceivers while
   eliminating their deceptions and dangers.
4. *Elaborate* on each of the three alternatives, and do so
   persuasively enough that readers will want to absorb and
   adopt them, and prescriptively enough that readers will
   understand how to do so.

We have now finished the first objective, and you have seen through the veneer of the joy thieves and are ready for better and truer alternatives. Next, it is important to have a good frame of reference for the three new attitudes or approaches to life that will be presented in the second side. A frame sets something off, holds it together, and presents it in its clearest and most attractive light. The framework for the alternatives will lead you through the change in attitudes needed for real happiness.

PARADIGMS

What are control, ownership, and independence? Are they goals? Are they principles? Are they attitudes? Are they approaches to life? Are they beliefs? Are they lenses through which we view the world? Are they ideals or idols which we worship?

It's hard to replace something if you are not entirely sure what it is. Like parts in an automobile or machine, you have to know what something is and where it goes and what it does before you can replace it correctly and accurately.

CO&I are not values or precepts, they are concepts or attitudes, and they are ultimately false.

The two steps to get rid of false concepts are, first, to debunk, expose, and abandon them (the purpose of side one of this book); and, second, to replace them (the purpose of side two).

A concept can be replaced only with an alternative concept. A paradox can be replaced with a paradigm. And what we need is a switch to go from one to the other.

THE HAPPINESS SWITCH AND THE MOTIVATION TO THROW IT

It would be great if there were a switch somewhere—on a wall or in your brain or on your heart—a switch with which you could literally turn on happiness.

While that kind of quick-flip switch doesn't exist, there is another kind of happiness switch that actually works—it is the switch from the paradox of control, ownership, and independence to the new paradigm of the three alternatives—the switch that takes you from building the container to filling it up.

It is not like a light switch; it is a much more complex switch that involves switching places, changing positions, transitioning from one viewpoint to another. It is a switch that requires you to turn your perspective upside down. It is a BIG switch, a hard one to throw, and it will take all your focus and determination.

The two strongest motivators are *love* and *fear*. And there is a good chance that both can come into play in finding and throwing the happiness switch.

You might ask: What is going to motivate me to make a switch that fundamental, that complete? You might say: Even if I become convinced that striving for control, ownership, and independence is working against my happiness and if I start to believe that there are some alternative attitudes that might work better—even if all that happens— what is going to motivate me to leave my mental comfort zone and to make the effort required to consciously change how I look at things, and to stop pursuing what I've thought I wanted all my life and start looking for something different?

It's a good question, and here is a hopeful answer: It has been said that the two strongest motivators are *love* and *fear*. And there is a good chance that both can come into play in finding and throwing the happiness switch.

The first half of this book has the goal of helping us develop a certain kind of fear—a fear of the false and unhappiness-producing pursuits of control, ownership, and independence. It is not enough simply to disclaim or disavow these deceivers, we need to actually develop a healthy fear of them, of what they can do to our lives, and how they can undermine our relationships, our spontaneity, and our humility.

Often, what can focus our fear is when we see excessive control, owner-ship, and independence in others. It's one thing to observe or criticize or try to deal with a control-freak, but it is something else—and potentially a very positive thing—to fear developing those instincts in ourselves. We all know people who are greedy and prideful in their ownership and it is healthy to fear those same tendencies in ourselves. And when we meet someone who never lets their guard down, never lets us see their vulnerability, and acts like all they need is themselves—we should fear letting those same attitudes grow in ourselves.

Encourage yourself to develop a healthy fear of CO&I. Notice it. Recognize it. Be wary of it. Prepare yourself to disavow and avoid it. That kind of fear is a powerful motivation and precursor for finding and adopting a different approach and a new paradigm.

Fear can be a powerful motivator, but here is even better news: the one motivation that is even stronger than fear, and certainly sweeter, is *love*. And the other side of this book has a single goal: to help you understand and grow to love the three alternatives.

The second side of this book is about love. It will help you to love the three alternatives—to love them as interesting and insightful concepts, to love them for the truth they entail, to love them for the new way they allow you to see life, and to love them for the changes they can make in what you pursue, what you value, and how you live.

Let fear and love work together and let them both motivate us to switch from the paradox to the paradigm.

—

CHAPTER 8

WHAT ARE THE THREE ALTERNATIVES?

What we need as replacements are three separate, new paradigms, one to replace each of the three deceivers or thieves of joy. We need three new ways to view the world around us, three new approaches to living out each day, three new frameworks in which we can see ourselves and our lives on this earth, three new ways of dealing with the materialism and shallowness and selfishness around us, three new attitudes to face each day.

THINGS AS THEY REALLY ARE

A true paradigm or set of paradigms would represent things as they really are—the realities of our frailty and our needs, of our dependence and interdependence. A true paradigm would allow us to see our best selves and also see others with an open mind. True paradigms would take into account our truest purpose. True paradigms would be frameworks in which all true principles could flourish.

The three alternatives should be a set of attitudes or perspectives or paradigms that make us better and happier.

Are there three paradigms that can motivate and inspire us and give us purpose and confidence yet keep us in the humility and receptive mode that allow us to draw down spiritual help and comfort? Can they contain the faith of seeing what can someday be, but also the humility to recognize how far we still have to go?

This is no small thing we are looking for together. We are seeking bridges that can allow us to live in the world without accepting all its values and assumed ideas. We are seeking attitudes that maximize our progression in life. We are seeking paradigms that rid us of false mindsets and point us toward lasting perspectives.

Before you turn the book over, formulate your own ideas for what the three alternatives are. Use these last three pages of this side to write down your speculations on the identity of the three joy rescuers.

I think the alternative to control is:

_____

Here's why:

_____

_____

_____

_____

_____

_____

_____

_____

_____

_____

_____

I think the alternative to ownership is:

_____

Here's why:

_____

_____

_____

_____

_____

_____

_____

_____

_____

_____

_____

I think the alternative to independence is:

_____

Here's why:

_____

_____

_____

_____

_____

_____

_____

_____

_____

_____

_____

_____

A BRIEF INTERMISSION AND TRANSITION

Most efforts at self-improvement work from outside-in. If we say "I need to simplify," our instinct is to start working on our schedule or our lifestyle or the kind of food we eat or on how we prioritize things.

If we say "I need to get in better shape," we set up an exercise program or drink a certain number of glasses of water per day or use our smartphones to keep track of how many steps we take or how high we get our heartbeat.

The assumption is that we can change how we think or how we feel by changing what we do, and to an extent that is true. We change something on our outside in the hopes that it will change us on the inside.

Our instinct is to focus on what we do rather than on what we are. We focus on the means instead of on the end.

What about the opposite approach? What about changing our inner attitudes and paradigms with the trust that if we change our inside, it will change us on the outside?

Ninety-nine percent of goals or plans or New Year's resolutions are about changing what we do. Very few are about changing what we think or how we think.

This book is about changing three inside attitudes in the belief that they will ultimately change everything about what we do and how we do it. Change the inside to change the outside. Change our paradigm to change our behavior and our approach and our outcome.

Change the paradigm to fix the paradox.

If your goal is to lose weight, of course you will need a plan for eating and for exercise—for working from the outside-in; but what if there was a particular internal attitude and paradigm that would motivate you to take care of your body in a way you never have before—that allowed you to change your physical self from the inside out?

If you want to be a better parent, you may start thinking in terms of what you can do to change your children (which is paradoxical to begin with) and indeed there are ways to work at parenting by modifying children's behavior and changing them from the outside-in; but what if there was another specific paradigm that would make you more patient, more spontaneous, and more aware of what your children really need—that would make you a better parent from the inside out?

If your objective is to have more money and live more comfortably, it is natural to set financial goals and to work harder and smarter and improve your circumstances from the outside-in; but what if there was a third paradigm that made you see things differently, recognize opportunities sooner, and work more effectively with other people—that would help you see wealth differently and become a more abundant person from the inside out?

These three inside-out paradigms really do exist and you are now ready to flip this book over and read about them.

END OF THE PARADOX.

PLEASE FLIP TO THE PARADIGM.

WAIT . . .

If you are opening this book from this side first, or if you have not yet read the other side, please STOP and turn the book over.

Read the three deceivers before you read the three alternatives.

Read about the happiness paradox before you read about the happiness paradigm.

Sequence is important!

And reading the solution before you understand the problem is confusing.

Read about the three joy thieves before you read about the three joy rescuers.

par·a·digm
A set of assumptions, concepts, values, and practices that constitutes a way of viewing reality. A model, pattern, template, or perspective—a worldview or a mental framework in which to see and understand what is around us.

Can we develop a paradigm path that leads us, consistently and reliably, toward the goal of happiness?

To restore what has been stolen,

to recover what has been lost,

to rescue ourselves from deception,

to undo the untruths that we have blindly accepted

and to replace them with what we had in the first place—

the attitudes and the antecedents of true happiness.

May we sail through the **parad ox**

And into the beauty of a new **parad igm**

And find that

Shifting from the **ox** to the **igm**

is the best move we have ever made.

That is the voyage of side two.

Richard Eyre

HOW A NEW VIEW
CAN TURN THINGS
RIGHT-SIDE UP

The
Happiness
Paradigm

CONTENTS

SYNERGICITY

LIVING THE NEW PARADIGM FOR HAPPINESS

FOREWORD

BY CHARLES RANDALL PAUL

I f you have followed the author's instructions you will not be surprised to be reading another preface because you will be effectively starting a new book—this time cleared of misconceptions, and open to learning better ways to think, feel, and act toward and in joyfulness. Although very practical in its focus, this is not a typical self-help book. It is a powerful testimony from the author's very full life of conscientious thought and experimentation with lasting happiness that actually endures the various difficulties of human existence.

Richard and Linda Eyre have traveled, learned, and taught frequently in Asia as well as the West. This text is a remarkable attempt to speak out of and to both the Eastern way of wisely being in the moment and the Western way of striving for a high future purpose. The Western way advocates obedience to God or rationality leading to a reward of eventual bliss in Heaven or on a utopian Earth, while the Eastern way teaches alignment with the Dharma allowing enlightenment that reality is already complete for those liberated from the illusion of identity and the desire for more. Richard concludes that the resistance between the two can provide strengthening leverage to each. In short, he suggests that we can enjoy the process of seeking on purpose. Neither being nor becoming can claim comprehensive Reality without the other.

replacing typical Western attitudes of control, ownership, and independence and Eastern attitudes of utter human inadequacy with a new paradigm that blends the two into a revolutionary new approach to happiness.

Joy is experienced or revealed in the love and creativity and humor and pathos of mutual friendships and loyal family relations that provide infinite surprises as humans originate new adventures together. This radical freedom of mutual influence is the essence of a spiritual relationship. Thus, Eyre's new happiness paradigm essentially lays out the ways we can respectfully engage over what is good or best in an ongoing contest of out-loving each other in creative original ways. That is what joyful beings do to become more joyful.

Richard hopes to inspire us to take each day joyfully but also seriously—asking and listening to the Higher Power and to each other—resisting real negative influencers—and accountably recording in writing our results. Not an easy project to pack into a few pages; but he did it. I trust readers will enjoy and employ this life-shifting prescription for sustained happiness.

— CHARLES RANDALL PAUL

Converting the Saints: A Study of Religious Rivalry in America

PREFACE

THE TWO SIDES OF A CHANGE

There are two steps to rid ourselves of false ideas or half-truths. First, we must *expose* them, dig down and discover where and why they are false, and consciously reject them and turn away from them. That was the task of side one.

The next step is to *replace* them with true and longer-perspective viewpoints—to push the old views aside by replacing them with new ways of looking at the world that fit better with both physical and spiritual reality and that lead us toward, rather than away from, happiness. This is the mission of side two.

THE CRITERIA

There are four important criteria on which the three alternatives are superior to the three deceivers:

1. *Truth*: They are correct principles, eternally valid and sound, while the deceivers build on half-truths and lead to conclusions that are ultimately false.
2. *Motivation*: The alternatives are more inspiring, and will stimulate more action and initiative than the deceivers.
3. *Love*: The alternatives open up and lead to giving and receiving more love.
4. *Happiness*: To the point and the title of this book—the three alternatives will produce not only more happiness, but a better *kind* of happiness.

Our unveiling of each of the three alternatives will first announce the word, then define it with an explanation to show how it meets the four criteria. Then each alternative will be contrasted with the deceiver that it replaces, justifying why it is more correct—more motivating—and why it produces more love and happiness.

THE PARADIGM SHIFT

There is a classic story of a ship at sea. The ship captain sees on his radar that he is on a collision course with another vessel. He radios the message that the other vessel should change course. The response is "No, you change course." Angry, the captain radios again, "I am a mega tanker and you are in my path; YOU change course."

The next response reveals the captain's false paradigm: "I am the lighthouse; YOU change course."

False paradigms happen often, on many levels and magnitudes. Early hospitals killed more people than they saved because they had a false paradigm

about what caused disease. Smoking was indulged and tolerated for centuries because of false paradigms about what it did for the body. Flight was thought impossible because of false paradigms about aerodynamics until that famous day at Kitty Hawk in 1903.

But it's the personal paradigms, the individual ways in which we see the world, and our purpose, and the means by which happiness is obtained that make the biggest difference for each of us.

And the unfortunate thing is that most of the false paradigms that we carry with us and pattern our lives around were not consciously and analytically figured out personally by each of us; rather, they were adopted from the "norms" around us.

We see having control, and acting rather than reacting, as good because society has judged it as good. We see ownership as the goal because everyone accepts it as a measurable reality and a basis for comparison. We see independence as the ideal because it is identified with strength and freedom whether it really has anything to do with those things or not.

Adopting the prevailing paradigm is the easy path. And the only way to break out of the pattern is to think hard, think spiritually, and think for yourself about the possibility that some of your paradigms are false and that they may need to be changed.

We need to allow for the possibility that our paradigms about where happiness comes from may be inaccurate, lead in an opposite direction, and may in fact be a paradox. Then we are free to find a better happiness paradigm.

OUR SIXTH SENSE, AND MY DEFINITION OF SPIRITUAL

As the three alternatives are presented and taken to their highest levels, the word *spiritual* will often be used and thus needs some explanation and definition.

We live in country and in a time when less than half of us describe ourselves as religious, but three-quarters of us describe ourselves as spiritual.

Spiritual means different things to different people, but the common thread is that most of us sense that there is more to us than our physical

bodies and brains—and that there are more ways of knowing things than through our five senses. We know there is something more, something higher, because we have felt it.

The three alternatives are new attitudes or approaches to life and to happiness that draw on and enhance our awareness, sensitivity, and powers of observation—through our five senses and through a sixth sense that I choose to call spiritual.

THE BIG REVEAL

It just so happens (well, actually some pretty hard work went into making it happen) that each of the three alternatives, or the three joy rescuers, is an eleven-letter word that starts with the letter *S*. By explaining them one at a time, the hope is to convince you to work hard at adopting the alternatives as the lenses through which you view yourself and your world—as the three rescuers of joy and as your personally chosen path to happiness. The chapters that follow will elaborate, expand, and give implementation suggestions on each of the alternatives. The goal here is simply to reveal and define them.

THE ALTERNATIVE TO CONTROL IS SERENDIPITY

This marvelous word has been adopted and oversimplified recently by popular culture, becoming the name of ice cream stores, boutiques, movies, and clothing lines. In its new popularity, *serendipity* is often defined as "fate" or "luck" or "having something good happen to you purely by chance." It's true definition though, is much more interesting and illuminating.

The word was coined by a nineteenth-century English author named Horace Walpole who loved an ancient Persian fable called *The Three Princes of Serendip*. Serendip was the early name of the beautiful, teardrop-shaped island off the southern tip of India that the British called Ceylon and that we, today, call Sri Lanka.

In the fable, each of the three princes sets out in search of his fortune. None of them actually find a fortune, but all of them, through their extraordinary awareness and perception, find things that are *better* than a fortune: They discover love, truth, and opportunities to serve. They are able to unearth these treasures because they notice things that other people miss and thus realize unexpected joys and discoveries.

Walpole, reading the fable, said to himself, "We do not have an English word that expresses that happy ability to find things that are better than what we think we are seeking." So, he made up the word *serendipity* and defined it as follows:

"A state of mind whereby a person, by good fortune and through awareness and sensitivity, frequently finds something better than that which he is seeking."

DEFINITION

Think for a moment about the elements and implications of Walpole's fascinating definition. First, it is a person's state of mind or attitude. Second, it requires awareness and sensitivity. Third, it implies that the person is proactive, because he or she is seeking things or has goals. Fourth, it suggests that, as life spontaneously happens, we get opportunities or impressions or ideas—perhaps related to things most people miss—that are actually better or more joyful than whatever we were consciously doing or seeking.

Walpole's definition implies that even as we live our lives, going about our business, controlling what we can, and pursuing our goals, *we should strive to stay aware and in tune,* using both our senses and our intuition or inspiration. As we do, we may well see better paths—things both more important and happier than what is on our to-do list.

These serendipities can be big or small. They might involve little opportunities or small beauties like an unexpected call from a friend or a lovely sunset. They can also be big connections or discoveries. For example, Alexander Fleming discovered antibiotics by the serendipitous observation of how the mold blown in through an open window started killing bacteria on a Petri dish in his lab. And Charles Goodyear figured out how to vulcanize rubber by noticing what happened when a pot boiled over on his stove.

On the micro or the macro level, the search for serendipity puts the premium not on controlling, but on observing. Our focus is not on forcing things to be the way we want them, but on seeing the possibilities in things as they really are.

Serendipitous, by the way, is the adjectival form—and a highly useful and descriptive word as we shall see.

SPIRITUAL SERENDIPITY

Serendipity gets even more interesting when the spiritual dimension is brought in. We can strive to be more aware and observant not only by way of our five senses, but also through our intuition and spiritual sensitivity. As we strive to become more attuned to the feelings of our soul, things come to us via impressions, nudges, promptings, hunches, and inspiration. Through these we become more in touch with what is really going on around us, and we begin to see things in a more complete and insightful way.

An enhanced, spiritual definition of *serendipity* would then be:

> A state of mind and spirit wherein we strive for awareness of divine blessings, purpose, and will. As we go about our lives and seek our goals, we try to notice all that is around us and inside us, happy for the adventure and spontaneity of life and willing to detour or depart from our plans each time we become aware of something better.

CONTRASTING THE DECEIVER WITH ITS ALTERNATIVE

Control or serendipity: Which is most true, which is most motivating, which best accommodates and attracts love, and which produces the most happiness?

Truth: The fact is that we control so very little—most is beyond and above our control; and yet unexpected opportunities, circumstances, and blessings are all around us, along with incredible beauties, and we need only the awareness and spiritual sensitivity to notice them. We can cultivate this awareness and we can ask for it. As we do, we use our agency to take the spiritual initiative that allows the divine to bless us in ways we could never have planned and to prompt us in directions we never would have contemplated. This kind of liminal guidance is infinitely more valuable and worthier of our desire than our own personal control. And *serendipity* is the mind-state or paradigm that can attract these gifts.

Motivation: Control can seem motivating because it appeals to our desire for power. But it is a dangerous kind of motivation because it is often unbridled by humility and can lead to the worst kind of pride. With a serendipity paradigm, we are motivated by our desire to discover happiness rather than trying to manufacture it all the time. We begin to see life as a great adventure where our challenge is not to control but to notice and perceive and understand. Serendipity also increases our resilience because, unlike control, it prompts us to look for the hidden opportunities, even in our defeats.

Love: Love has many definitions, but all involve care and concern and deep feelings for others, each of which is fostered more by the awareness of serendipity than by the self-focused elevation of control.

Happiness: The results of a control paradigm can include obsessive behavior and a lot of stress and frustration from all the situations and circumstances (and people) in life that simply don't happen the way we want them to. In a control mentality, we are annoyed by surprises or unexpected occurrences that distract us from the things on our list. Things that don't fall into line with our plans and our controlling idea of how things should happen are seen as interruptions, irritations, impediments.

> With a serendipity paradigm, we are motivated by our desire to discover happiness rather than trying to manufacture it all the time.

The results of a spiritually serendipitous paradigm are happier, more peaceful, and much more exciting. Through our increased awareness, we learn to live in the moment and enjoy the present. We do our best to plan our future, but we relish spontaneity and become good at expecting and looking for surprises and unplanned opportunities. We take off the blinders of our obsessions. With our peripheral vision restored, we notice both the needs and the beauties of others.

A serendipitous attitude seems to slow time down, take the pressure off, and make us observers rather than feverish little worriers trying to control our own little imagined world, and continually failing to do so.

While a control approach closes the inner door, a serendipitous approach opens us to our own souls.

We were living in suburban Washington, DC, where I had cofounded a highly successful political consulting company, planning and managing the campaigns of candidates in gubernatorial, senatorial, and congressional races. I liked the excitement and potential contribution of what I was doing and had some political ambitions of my own; but the pace was exhausting, I was traveling three or four days a week, and Linda and I were worried about our three small children and trying to decide what kind of preschool experience they needed.

I was still preoccupied with my study of joy, and thought there ought to be an alternative to the pushy academics of the preschools in our area that were promising to teach three-year-olds to read and do math and be way ahead of other kids when they got to kindergarten. We started writing our ideas down and before long had the basis of a book that we called Teaching Children Joy, *which suggested that preschoolers were better off and more prepared for school by learning social and emotional joys—like the joy of kindness, the joy of simple goal setting, the joy of the earth and the body—than by getting a head start academically. I started to feel that my heart was more in the book than in political consulting and I began to cut back my time with the company so Linda and I could expand our writing. I didn't fully realize it at the time, but I was behaving serendipitously, moving off of my goals and going toward "something better than that which I had been pursuing." Long story short: The book became a bestseller and spawned a Joy School curriculum, which has now been used by more than half a million parents with their preschoolers (see JoySchools.com).*

THE ALTERNATIVE TO OWNERSHIP IS STEWARDSHIP

DEFINITION

This is an old word, dating back to the eleventh century. *Webster* says it "functioned as a job description, denoting the office of a steward, or manager of a large household," implying the watchful care of something we do not own. *Webster* again: "the careful and responsible management of something entrusted to one's care."

More recently, the word has found extensive use in business as in the "stewardship theory" of management where executives act as responsible stewards of the assets they control. We also hear a lot lately about "environmental stewardship" referring to responsibility and protection of the natural environment through conservation and sustainable practices.

And the word has long had a spiritual connotation. According to Wikipedia, "Stewardship is a theological belief that humans are responsible for the world, and should take care of it . . . In Jewish, Christian, and Muslim traditions, stewardship refers to the way time, talents, material possessions, or wealth are used or given for the service of God."[7]

Stewardship is the understanding that we really own nothing and that things merely pass through us and through our lives—things we can care for, take responsibility for, and find joy in.

I like to define *stewardship* as

A paradigm in which one feels full responsibility for something he knows he is not fully deserving of—something both worked-for and received, for which we feel dedication and passion—something which brings us a sense of magnifiable and expanding gratitude and joy which we want to share with others.

Stewardship implies that we are taking care of what we are entrusted with, by the true owner and for the greater good. In this attitude, we perceive responsibility, but neither greed nor pride can flourish. A stewardship paradigm brings with it a natural humility and gratitude that lead us toward happiness.

SPIRITUAL STEWARDSHIP

Another way to grasp the difference between ownership and stewardship is, as was briefly alluded to earlier, to think of them as the trunks of two trees and to observe the limbs that grow on each.

On the ownership tree, there is a jealousy limb and an envy limb and a coveting limb, because ownership is always comparing and competing, and it is easy to constantly notice those who have more than we do. There is also a condescension limb, a pride limb, and a superiority limb, because it is also easy to see those who have less than we do. And there are selfish limbs and frustration limbs and over ambitious limbs because we want to climb over others so we can look down on them instead of right into their eyes.

There are also some good branches on the tree—such as a responsibility branch because we are motivated to take care of things we feel ownership of. Even branches of charity and giving can sprout, but they are often choked out by the strong selfish limbs.

On the stewardship tree, very different kinds of branches tend to grow, such as healthy humility branches and reaching limbs of thanksgiving. Appreciation branches sprout for the beauty and opportunity and options that life gives us. Strong empathy limbs grow for the pains and challenges of others. Limbs for prayer and faith and hope are inevitable, because they are principles by which stewardships are honored, fulfilled, and magnified. Branches of charity intertwine with the limbs of love and of sensitivity, because we know things are not ours anyway, so it is much easier to share them with others.

This kind of tree, and this kind of growth, is the result of living a life with a stewardship attitude.

CONTRASTING THE DECEIVER WITH ITS ALTERNATIVE

Ownership or stewardship: Which is most true, which is most motivating, which brings the most love, and which produces the most happiness?

Truth: Ownership can be true economically, but stewardship is the greater truth emotionally and spiritually. It's true in a bigger way, a more caring way, a less selfish way. It is true in a higher awareness and perspective.

Motivation: There is no question that ownership is motivating. But it is a motivation that is varying and vulnerable because greed can consume itself and become exhausting rather than renewing. Stewardship's motivation is warmed and sustained by gratitude where we see what we have as gifts beyond what we have worked for or deserve. Those with a stewardship mentality want more stewardship, just as owners want more ownership, but they want it less for pride and appearance and more for love and service and the common good. In stewardship, motivation is more peaceful.

> Stewardship carries a deeper sense of joy than ownership, because it couples with gratitude rather than with pride.

Love: Ownership turns one inward, stewardship outward. Stewardship opens opportunities for sharing and service which bring feelings of love and appreciation; while ownership hoards and hides.

Happiness: The quantity of results is potentially endless with ownership, but the happiness that comes with it follows the law of diminishing returns. Each time you get another something it produces less satisfaction than the last time. Owning much can be become tiresome. With stewardship, quality gradually becomes more important than quantity, and we learn that it is possible to be happy and content without being satisfied. Stewardship carries a deeper sense of joy than ownership, because it couples with gratitude rather than with pride.

Just after writing the Joy School book, we were offered a three-year hiatus from our companies to go to London and supervise the humanitarian activities of the several hundred young missionaries volunteering full time and working with refugees and others, mostly in the poor areas of London and Southern England. This was a calling *and not a job, and it paid nothing. It would mean leaving both our consulting company and our writing and publishing, and there was no guarantee that we could pick either of them back up when we returned. Our "ownership" and our income would take a hit, our kids would be uprooted from their schools, and we would live much more simply in a smaller house in a new and somewhat foreign culture. But Linda and I both felt strongly that this was a stewardship, that we could really change lives, both of the missionaries and of the people they could serve and help. It caused us to look at everything else as a stewardship as well, from the houses and cars we would have to sell or rent to our children and the type of experience and perspective we wanted to give them. The more we thought about it the more we knew that this was both a stewardship and a serendipity. It was something better than what we had been seeking, and it was a way to pursue contribution over personal prosperity. We did it, and those three years changed our perspective, our ambitions, and our life story.*

THE ALTERNATIVE TO INDEPENDENCE IS SYNERGICITY

The third alternative is an attitude that not only pulls us out of the deceptive and negative clutches of the false concept of independence, it also complements (and attracts) serendipity and stewardship.

It required the coining of a new word, and that word is *synergicity*. As many will quickly recognize, it is a combination of two other words, *synergy* and *synchronicity*.

Synergy—the first half of our new word—is an important (and current-
ly very popular) concept meaning the combination of two or more people,
approaches, or points of view, where the total is greater than the sum of its
parts. One plus one can equal three, two plus two can equal five—or more.
When two people or groups or companies or concepts complement each
other, or motivate each other in certain ways, the combined result can be
much greater than the aggregate of what each could do separately.

DEFINITION

The word actually comes from the Greek word *synergos*, which means
working together. The dictionary defines *synergy* as "A mutually advantageous conjunction where the whole is greater than the sum of the parts. A
dynamic state in which combined action is favored over the sum of individual component actions."

While the word *synergy* is used a lot in business, its best use may be in
human relationships, particularly in marriage. A husband and wife, working together with complementing skills and perspectives, should produce a
synergistic marriage that accomplishes much more than the total of what the
two individuals could do on their own.

But we need something more. *Synergy* lacks the amazing, cosmic, perfect-
timing quality where things fit magically together.

It lacks the quality of *synchronicity*.

Synchronicity is a term made up by Carl Jung, the Swiss psychiatrist known
for his exploration of the subconscious mind. He used the word to describe
what he called "temporally coincident occurrences of acausal events." Jung
variously described synchronicity as an "acausal connecting principle" (i.e.,
a pattern of connection that cannot be explained by direct causality—a
"meaningful coincidence") and as "acausal parallelism"[8] (things that happen together and in tandem without apparent linkage). It differs from mere
coincidence in that synchronicity implies not just a happenstance, but an
underlying pattern or dynamic expressed through meaningful relationships
or events.

Jung may not have appreciated the spiritual connections, or realized that there are outside-the-mind causes for these things that seem to go beyond coincidence, but his word is fascinating because it begins to give us a way to talk about those amazing moments when everything just seems to converge—when the whole universe seems to plot together and coalesce for our happiness or well-being. It suggests the interconnectedness of the micro and the macro, like butterflies flapping their wings in Brazil and affecting the climate in New York City; or the thought and reality connections of someone calling you just at the moment you were thinking of him.

When you add the spiritual dimension, synchronicity becomes a way to talk about the amazing timing of God's tender mercies in our lives and the connections between the thoughts and feelings of loved ones that can't be explained in cause-and-effect terms. It teaches us that "coincidence" is a word we use when we don't notice the divine in things. And when you link spiritual synchronicity with spiritual synergy, you get our remarkable new word: *synergicity*—the perfect antidote and alternative to independence.

Instead of looking for ways to do better than others, it aims at ways of doing better with others.

Synergicity is a rescuer and restorer of joy rather than a destroyer. Instead of saying that we must stand alone, it says that in most aspects of life, we are completely dependent on higher, more spiritual forces. Instead of implying that we don't need others, it suggests that we are all interdependent and that people working together can accomplish much more than the total of what they could do separately.

Synergicity focuses on family, friends, relationships, communities—and on connecting everything to the greater whole. Instead of looking for ways to do better than others, it aims at ways of doing better with others. Instead of striving to do things in spite of the circumstances around us, it prompts us to do things within and in harmony with the realities that surround us. And in its most spiritual dimension, instead of the goal of lifting ourselves by our bootstraps to the objectives we have set, it suggests letting God lift us to our divine destinies.

Synergicity is a lens through which we try to view the world more organically—with everything interconnected, everything benefiting from and interdependent with everything else.

Synergicity then, the third and final alternative, is

A combination of the words *synergy* and *synchronicity* defined as a paradigm in which we acknowledge divine dependence, mutual interdependence, and respect for the beneficial interconnectedness of all things, times, and occurrences within the framework of a higher purpose.

SPIRITUAL SYNERGICITY

The key to implementing an attitude of synergicity is to understand that, while our perspective and grasp of reality is narrow and limited by our veiled mortality, we have three incredible tools at our disposal, each of which can open things up to us and give us a broader view of the larger reality. These tools, that our souls or spirits can access, are:

1. Our own brains. We use less than 10 percent of the capacity of our marvelous minds. The power of our subconscious is largely untapped. We can program our brains to show us connections, to notice subtle things, to put the right words into our mouths, or prompt the comment or the complement that someone else needs. We can literally tell our minds to be more aware, to nudge us to call someone when they are available, or to remember things from past experience that are relevant to what we are doing at the moment.

2. Other people's consciousness. When we ask other people how they feel, how they see things, what their take is, it's like getting a whole new picture with a whole new camera angle. When we develop our sense of empathy,

we can sometimes get these perspectives without even asking. The point is that there is so much awareness and perspective around us, in the form of other people with their own sets of experiences and viewpoints, and the more we tap into them, the more our own awareness and perspective expands.

3. A higher spiritual power. We can develop spiritual connection to a more comprehensive grasp of all reality, wherein we have the awesome privilege of access to a higher perspective. This connection is a gift, but it is one we can work for and ask for and learn to recognize.

Think of these three resources in a technology metaphor. Our brains are our laptops or smartphones, which have far more capacity and memory and connections than we normally use.

Other people's experience and insights and perspectives are our connections and apps and social media—but without the false and the fake. By connecting and tapping in, we dramatically expand our own computer's speed, access, memory, and capacity.

And the spiritual is the internet and Wi-Fi and Google, the unlimited database—the endless capacity source to which we have access and which never breaks down or goes offline.

CONTRASTING THE DECEIVER WITH ITS ALTERNATIVE

As we did with the other two alternatives of serendipity and stewardship, let's compare, on the same four criteria, synergicity with independence.

Truth: Independence is simply not an accurate paradigm. To reiterate, as hard as we might try to convince ourselves that we are independent, we are actually completely dependent on this earth, and its spirit for everything that keeps us alive, and interdependent with so many other people. Synergicity recognizes this simple truth and turns it into a magnificent blessing.

Motivation: The self-centering notion of trying to do everything our-selves, to stand alone, to depend only on self, is a stubborn and defensive kind of motivation. It is likely to burn out and turn brittle. The motivation of synergicity reaches out, and has the excitement of lifting others as it lifts us, and the adventure of trying to fit the pieces of life's puzzle together.

Love: Unlike independence, synergicity expands the number of things we can love, and makes the love of special people vast and exciting in the possibility of becoming, together, more than twice what either can be alone. It invites more into the circle of love, more people, more ideas, more experiences.

Happiness: Independence, doing things with only our own capacity and our narrow perspective, has the potential of only very limited, and often highly unhappy, results. Synergicity, and finding the connections that are all around us magnifies every joy and extends every potential—all limits are off.

After our return from England, where two more children were added to our family, Linda and I settled back into our writing and speaking niche and wrote Lifebalance *and later another book that became a* New York Times *#1 bestseller—*Teaching Your Children Values. *We were on* Oprah *and the* Today Show *and for a while did a regular segment on* CBS This Morning. *We had an ongoing five-book contract with Simon & Schuster. With the decision to close down our consulting company, we become full-time writers and speakers. We didn't realize it at the time, but the most important thing we were learning was synergicity. In our writing, we found that when we wrote together, we could produce more (and better) material than the total of what we each could do individually. Our skills and writing styles complemented each other, and we catalyzed them with brainstorming sessions with a writers' group we called "Inklings" in honor of C. S. Lewis.*

I began to realize that Linda had gifts I would never have, and that we were better off complementing and compensating for each other's strengths and weaknesses rather than trying to work inde-pendently. We learned to tie what we were writing and speaking

about to what was going on in the world and became better at seeing connections between what people needed and what was happening— and at changing the timing of what we were working on to match the opportunities that presented themselves. We started seeing that we were happiest when we felt that our work was a cause and that our possessions were stewardships. We began to trust unexpected opportunities and serendipity more than our own long-range planning. And we had learned how dependent our happiness and our productivity were on our interdependence with others and on our efforts to see the connections within the big picture. We were beginning not only to understand this third joy rescuer, but to see how it linked with and drove the other two.

Now, with the three alternatives defined, we can compare them as a new, three-cornered paradigm (SS&S) with the three deceivers (CO&I) that they replace. Once we have done that, we can delve deeper into each of the three alternatives—the three joy rescuers.

THE ROBBERS (CO&I) VERSUS THE RESCUERS (SS&S)

It is one thing to compare each of the three deceivers individually with its replacement alternative, but it is something else again to compare them collectively—to compare the paradox with the paradigm.

As we compare, remember that the point of this book is not to argue that the alternatives are morally superior to the deceivers (though that could be argued), or to promise that we will get further and succeed more with the alternatives than with the deceivers (although we generally do). The point is more stark and more straightforward. Simply, the three alternatives make us *happier* than the three deceivers. The paradigm is a straight, clear path toward happiness while the paradox is a confusing, winding path away from it.

This is not a book about character or achievement or success, though it refers to those things. It is a book about happiness. Hence, the three deceivers and the three alternatives are always addressed in that context—will they or won't they make us happy?

One good way to evaluate and compare their potential or propensity to make us happy is to list the times or situations when we recognize happiness, and then evaluate whether each of these correlates more with CO&I or with SS&S.

As I have perused the current happiness literature (and there is a lot of it), it seems to me that most happiness theories agree on the kinds of circumstance and experience that are most likely to produce happiness. I have tried to extrapolate ten of these:

1. When we are feeling genuine gratitude. Happiness equates almost perfectly with thankfulness. I have written in another book that I believe "gratitude is not the path to happiness, gratitude IS happiness in its most obtainable form."[9]

2. When we have those little, unpredictable joy moments that just suddenly and unexpectedly happen to us. It could be a surprise or an epiphany or just a peaceful instant when an acute little stab of happiness hits us. And just as we become aware of it, it passes.

3. When a wave of joy envelops us on a particular occasion or in a certain situation. These may come at a wedding, a graduation, or a promotion, sometimes from something as simple as a quiet evening at home, or a family dinner when you look around the table and feel a penetrating happiness washing over you—and it lasts more than a moment.

4. When we have a powerful feeling of love. The intensity of the love we are feeling usually matches perfectly with the intensity of our joy.

5. When we are giving or performing service. When helping others, or giving assistance, we are likely to feel a distinct form of happiness.

6. When we are experiencing adventure. While it might more accurately be called a "thrill," there is a connection between happiness and new experience, discovery, or adventure.

7. When we are in nature or in touch and contact with the natural world.

8. When we are temporarily removed from pressure, tension, and anxiety. There is a happy relief when we go somewhere or do something that disconnects us from comparing ourselves and competing with each other and feeling overworked and out of balance.

9. When we emerge from a crisis or dark time in our lives, and by contrast feel relieved and happy that it is over or that we got through it.

10. When our highest priority relationships are going well.

Using these ten as a template, I invite you to do your own evaluation. Think through your first impressions of how each of these ten happiness factors are impacted and affected by the common CO&I paradox. Then, consider how the alternative paradigm of SS&S would impact these situations. Which of the two lends itself best to our perceived happiness-moments, the rush and pressure of the three thieves or the awareness and peace of the three rescuers? Which attitudes do you most associate with these ten types of happiness?

1. W,hich is the best attitudinal atmosphere for gratitude, the I-deserve-it mentality of control ownership and independence or the everything-is-a-gift viewpoint of serendipity, stewardship, and synergy?

2. Which paradigm gives us the most awareness and perspective of what is happening in and around us right now and is thus most likely to notice and embrace the little moments of joy—the hard charging, outwork-my-colleagues of CO&I attitude or the more reflective, spontaneous paradigm of SS&S?

3. Which makes us most mindful or present and most receptive to the wash of joy at special occasions—the on-to-the-next-thing-in-my-world approach of focusing on a to-do list or the openness and exceeded expectations of the three alternatives?

4. Which allows unselfish, unconditional love to flourish best, the walled-off, "me-ness" of independence or the empathy of stewardship?

5. Which paradigm prompts more desire and capacity for service to others, the self-centered focus of CO&I or the extra-centeredness of SS&S?

6. Which leads us more into the adventure and experience of the unknown, the conservative, protective status quo of the three deceivers or the curious and courageous attitude of serendipity? Which of the two values and anticipates adventure and surprise; and which is threatened by them?

7. Which is most likely to escape the work world and notice and capture the beauty of the natural world, the check-off mentality of the joy thieves or the pause-and-think-and-ask-why mantra of the joy rescuers?

8. Which relaxes the pressure and stress, the prove-yourself-over-and-over approach of the deceivers or the more-about-others-than-about-me sense of the alternatives?

9. Which paradigm provides a comforting, perspective-filled mentality when we are dealing with a difficult time or a life-crisis? Which allows us to feel less alone, more connected, and more resilient, the warm blanket of the interdependent approach of the SS&S rescuers or the fragile rug of the CO&I robbers that can so quickly be pulled out from under us?

10. Which paradigm strengthens relationships as the highest priority, and which weakens them?

You may want to come back and revisit these ten questions after you finish this side of the book—come back with a fuller understanding of the joy rescuers and how they impact the ten factors connected to happiness.

A simple way to think of this book as you move further into the paradigm side is in the framework of ends and means. The end (the goal, the purpose, the destination) is JOY, and the means (the plan, the path, the attitude) is SERENDIPITY, STEWARDSHIP, and SYNERGICITY.

SERENDIPITY

THE PROMISE

(Serendipity's Impact)

What's needed is an attitude,
An attitude that can change the way we see life
and the way we *live* life.
It is an attitude that involves new awareness,
new approaches,
and a fresh answer
to the deepest and oldest personal questions
of how spiritual guidance is obtained.

We ask: How do we avail ourselves of the
insight, impressions, intuitions, and inspirations
that our belief in an interested higher power tells us must be
possible?
"Ask for it" goes the short answer (and the *good* answer).
But to be effectual,
asking must be accompanied by an awareness,
an approach, an *attitude*
that helps us ask the right questions and then
hear (and see)
the unexpected answers.
What is this attitude?
It is *Serendipity*.

Serendipity is not a program
or a technique or a method
or "six steps" or a "sequence of actions."
It's not about how to do something
or even about what to do.
In fact,

it doesn't have to do with doing.
It has to do with
Being.
And the changes it advocates are not *out* in our actions,
but *in*, in our souls.
A new attitude, deeply understood, does more than change
what we do. It becomes a part of us and thus
it changes who we are.

The attitude of Serendipity requires shifts in our paradigm
or worldview.
It suggests a new way of looking at ourselves,
our world,
and our relationship with the spiritual.

Serendipity, besides opening us to greater guidance, can:

- Relax us, reducing frustration and stress
- Increase life's excitement, remove boredom
- Sensitize us to beauty, deepen our feelings, and
- Increase the times when we feel moved
- Orient us to ideas and increase our creativity
- Make us more *people*-oriented (less *thing*-oriented)
- Enhance our sense of humor—
- Let us see more of life's little humorous ironies
- Make us more flexible, more spontaneous, more *fun*
- Give us more resilience
- Make our life longer (time *seems* to slow down for those
  who are highly observant and aware—and a calm spirit
  contributes to longevity)

Add the list together and
we are infused with Peace and Joy.

THE ORIGIN OF SERENDIPITY, A PERSONAL VIEW

There was a time, a specific time, when I became so enamored (some would say obsessed) with the idea of serendipity that I took a journey of discovery and research to try to understand the full meaning and implications of the word. The journey led me to the British Museum in London and then to Sri Lanka, a beautiful island off the southern tip of India (an island once called Serendip).

The story of what led up to this journey is a little embarrassing as well as painful. I was in my mid-twenties and had experienced just enough success to be dangerous (and arrogant). I had just finished my MBA at the Harvard Business School where my favorite professor, who we will call Professor Livingstone, had strong attitudes and

mantras like "Act, don't react" and "Never be surprised, because if
you are surprised it means that you failed to do sufficient contingen-
cy planning." I thought he walked on water and he made me feel so
independent that I didn't take any of the jobs or positions that were of-
fered; instead, with two partners, I started a political consulting firm
in Washington, DC. I thought I was in charge and had control, and I
thought I had earned it. I wanted power. I was insufferable.

But there was another side to me. I had spent an internship summer
in Hawaii where I worked for an airline and could fly for free. I liked
to go to the Big Island on weekends and hitchhike around. On one trip
I got a morning ride with a native Hawaiian couple who called them-
selves Rusty and Honey. I was trying to hitchhike from Kona to Hilo,
a long, winding journey in those days. I thought I would have to get
many different rides. But Rusty and Honey just kept going, stopping
periodically to get out and show me a waterfall or volcano or, at one
stop, Honey's grandparents' graves. At first, I was a little impatient
(my nature), but we were heading in the right direction. Rusty and
Honey were like children showing me all their favorite toys, explain-
ing everything to me in their broken English . . . and finally, as the sun
was setting, we pulled into Hilo.

I said something about being lucky that they were going all the way
to Hilo, and Rusty, looking confused, said, "Oh, no, we not going Hilo;
we going grocery store." Then I was the one who looked confused, so he
went on with the shrug of one stating the obvious, "We can go grocery
store tomorrow, can't take you Hilo tomorrow!"

It made such an impression on me that I spent most of the following year
pondering what seemed to me like life's core dilemma: Did I want to be like
Professor Livingstone or did I want to be like Rusty and Honey? Did I want
to be purposeful or free? Did I want power or spontaneity? Did I want to act
or react?

Part of that personal dilemma stemmed from some pretty blunt feed-
back I had received from a couple of friends and associates (and one
girlfriend) who were frank enough to tell me how controlling and

manipulative they thought I was. I will spare you the specifics, but phrases like "it's not all about you" and "you can't step on other people to get where you want to go" come to mind.

The other dilemma-prompter was that I had this mental picture of Rusty and Honey lingering in my mind, and they looked happier than Professor Livingstone.

I began to ask some deeply personal questions: Why did I want what I wanted? To what end? Why did I want more control? Was it an end in itself or did I think it would make me . . . happier?

It was sometime during this year-long dilemma that, quite by chance, I came upon the word serendipity. *It was the name of a folk singing group, The Serendipity Singers, and while their music didn't impress me much, the odd word hung in my mind long enough for me to look it up in an old unabridged dictionary in the university library.*

I must have been in a rare, reflective mood, because the definitions I found that day made me wonder if this word, this concept, was the solution to my Rusty-and-Honey-or-Livingstone dilemma. The note that I made in my journal that day read like this, "Serendipity is a case or situation in which one discovers something better than that which he was seeking."

Maybe, I thought for the first time, I can be both Rusty/Honey and Livingstone. I can seek and set goals and control and succeed like Livingstone and I can watch for spontaneous situations where I can wind down, let life happen, and just be.

I didn't really grasp the total concept, but I liked the notion of it. I liked the "both" of it. It wasn't until I read the full, historic definition of the word from the man who coined it that I knew I was truly on to something. To Horace Walpole, the British author who invented the word, serendipity was not about luck or fate, it was about *a state of mind:* a state of mind whereby, through awareness and sensitivity, one frequently finds something better than that which he is seeking.

That was the state of mind I wanted, and it led me on an odyssey of discovery.

THE TRIP TO SERENDIP

In this chapter, and in some of those to follow, my writing will become somewhat more personal as I share thoughts, journal quotes, and other personal observations from my individual quest for serendipity. I will sometimes write in broken lines or poetic format to emphasize the new alignment of thought that I was experiencing and to try to nudge your thought process into new perspectives. I want to use any device I can (different format, uneven lines, poetic layout, even notes and quotes from my diary) to cause you to read in a little different manner—and thus think in a new and perhaps more creative way. Come with me on this journey of discovery of the first joy rescuer.

JOURNAL: EXCERPTS FROM SRI LANKA

As I write, I'm sitting on the veranda of my room in Sri Lanka, looking out through the jungle toward the beach, watching a man lead his elephant into the sea for a bath.

Perhaps it is a rather extreme approach, but I've come here, halfway around the world, to a teardrop-shaped island in the Indian Ocean to find the origin, and perhaps the deeper meaning, of my favorite word.

Serendipity is an attitude of mind that can give us the means to move from where we are to where we want to be. More importantly, when we include spiritual input in its definition, it can help us move from where we are to where God wants us to be.

The word isn't mine; it was coined by an eighteenth-century British author named Horace Walpole. But you might say I have adopted it, and I dare say it may have come to mean more to me than it did to Walpole.

Walpole, the son of the British prime minister and a writer of gothic novels, had come across an ancient Persian fable called The Three

Princes of Serendip, *and he was fascinated by the implications of the story.*

I found the actual, original fable—one of the few copies left in the world—in the rare book library of the British Museum in London and retranslated it into modern English. But before we get into that, let me make a comment, based in part on the perspective I feel as I look at our world from this faraway place.

We live in a unique time and culture that is more challenging, more complex, and more competitive than that of any other era in history. Compared to people of other societies and times, our lives are bountiful, as well as busy, but they are always demanding and never predictable. No matter what course we choose, life is filled with surprises and unexpected turns in the road.

The stress and frustration most of us feel traces both to the demands and to the unpredictability. About the time that we seem to have an idea of where we're going or what we're doing, something comes along (a crisis, a change, a challenge, a circumstance) and suddenly we're in uncharted waters and often over our heads.

The problems we face are too diverse to have a single answer, unless that answer is an attitude—an attitude that can give guidance to life, turn adversity into advantage, impatience into insight, competition into charity, boredom into beauty. I call this attitude serendipity.

It is fashionable today to be in control, in charge, to plan and manage and even manipulate. We like to say act; don't react. But the fact is that we know so little and control so little. Surprises happen every day. And there are so many big things and small things over which we have no control. The fact is that on our own we don't know enough about the future, or about those around us, or even about ourselves, to consistently choose what is best for ourselves and others.

But we have the capacity to see more, to notice more, to find better ways, and there is a higher intelligence which knows more. There is a guide which can prompt and lead through small, sometimes

hard-to-notice, feelings and insights that we call nudges or impressions or intuitions or inspirations. Something about the beauty and pace and peace of this island helps me to know there is a higher and more joyful way, and I have chosen to call it serendipity.

Serendipity, to me, is an attitude that increases our receptivity to our own senses and our own minds and to a purer intelligence. With it, we can discard the futile goal of a totally self-managed life and adopt the goal of a guided life.

By this point, I was not only traveling to Sri Lanka in search of my favorite word's origin, I was writing articles about it and promoting it as an attitude I felt people needed more of. My wife, Linda, wrote a preface to one of those articles that carries some interesting insight:

Richard's fascination with the word and concept of serendipity began during our courtship and kind of peaked about the time of our first child's birth. Richard wanted to call our new daughter Serendipity, but I discouraged him with the observation that kids might call her Dipity. Still, the best I could get was a compromise and we named her Saren. Except for the fact that there is a nerve gas by that name; and except that the shortened dictionary definition of serendipity is "a happy accident"; and except for the fact that everyone calls her Sara or Sharon, I guess that she feels okay about her name. I remember one baby shower gift—an embroidered blanket labeled "Saren Wrap." I'm just glad she wasn't a boy, or Richard would have wanted to name him after the English author who coined the word—Horace!

Seriously though, bear with Richard and his strange terminology. My husband is a little weird in a lot of appealing ways, and I've come to appreciate his word almost as much as he does. It means, at least in our minds, a lot of powerful things and stands for a way of living (and a way of thinking) that is thrilling in terms of what it does to our day-to-day lives.

THE ISLAND, THE PEOPLE, THE CONTRAST, AND THE CHANGE

Sri Lanka means "resplendent isle"; I must say it is well named. As I looked out over that emerald green, high-mountained island in the indigo-blue Indian Ocean, I found hints to this puzzle of serendipity not only in the scenery but also in the people.

I saw workers fortunate if they earned two hundred rupees per week (about ten dollars). With that (and the fish they caught or the rice they grew), they fed large families. Yet, as in many poorer parts of the world, faces reflected more joy than discouragement. Nowhere have I seen a higher ratio of smiling, open faces, childlike in the positive sense that they never looked away from my eyes. Their own glances seemed layered with light.

Their faces looked out with no self-consciousness and invited me to look right back in. The concerns here were as simple as they were severe: food to eat, a roof and shelter in the monsoon season, some health care, and education for the children. Sri Lankans are an intelligent, joyful people. Most returning tourists come back as much for the people as for the perfect beaches and cool, jungle mountains.

Because the pace was slow, and the contrasts vivid (and because my favorite word was born here), this was a good place to think about the three princes and Horace Walpole. And it was an especially objective place from which to look back and think about our world of Western civilization in the early parts of the twenty-first century with all of its attendant stress and anxiety.

Our world is boisterously busy and confusingly complex. Options, opportunities, and obligations proliferate and grow like grass. Many of our problems stem from surplus rather than scarcity.

Our windows today are still rectangular and made of glass, but they are turned on and off with a switch or face-recognition and change their view with a swipe of our finger—they show us our competitors and make us materialistic, conjuring new wants and then disguising them as needs.

We find that trying to do it all and have it all and be it all won't work. Because there's not time. In fact, there's rarely a moment for any *choose to dos*

because we are too busy and preoccupied with the *have to dos*, and the red tape and responsibilities swallow up the tiny time allotment of the every day.

We try to prepare, to prioritize, and to plan. We make our lists and try to control the events that swirl around us, but nothing ever goes quite as we planned. Impediments and interruptions knock us off course and turn our planners into testaments of our failures.

Work and family and personal needs jerk at each other like a three-way tug of war. We look around us and seek comfort (or at least company) in the fact that everyone has the same stress, the same frustration, the same unbalance.

Part of the problem is that, woven in and wound around our society's accepted thinking, is the dangerously stiff and brittle thread of *quantity*.

—

We measure (and are measured) more by how much we do than
by how well we do it;
More by explicit external exhibit than by invisible internal
insight;
More by our breadth than by our depth;
More on our doing and our getting than on our being;
More on quantity than on quality.

So how do we change this system, this society? We don't!
What we change is our susceptibility to it, our stereotyped
subscription to its standard, our dependence on its approval.
What we change is ourselves.

And the tool that can turn and time and tune the transition is an
attitude of
Serendipity.

—

CHAPTER 2

—

HORACE WALPOLE AND THREE PERSIAN PRINCES

A good first step in trying to grasp the concept of Serendipity is to explore the word itself, its origin and definition. To do that, we need to go back nearly three hundred years to that English author named Horace Walpole, often referred to by his friends as Harry. The following overview on Walpole is taken from my earlier book *Spiritual Serendipity*.

OVERVIEW

Walpole, in a letter written in 1754 to Horace Mann, commented on his attraction to the life adventures of the princes of Serendip: "They

were always making discoveries, by accident and by sagacity, of things of value . . . that they were not in quest of."[10]

What type of man was this Walpole? Did his interest in the concept of serendipity and his intrigue with a fanciful fable called *The Three Princes of Serendip* spring from the kind of person he was?

Walpole was born in 1717, the son of Sir Robert Walpole, who would later become England's prime minister. He grew up a son of privilege and leisure, a product of Eton and Kings College, Cambridge. Leaving the university, he set out on a two-and-a-half-year tour of France. While he was abroad, his father had him elected to Parliament. His life was the epitome of the blessings of noble birth in eighteenth century England; however, rather than complacency and laziness, Walpole seemed to derive productivity and widespread interests from his privilege.

Antiquary, novelist, politician, poet-master, social charmer, architect, gardener, and political chronicler all became appropriate descriptions for Walpole. Always appreciative of the unique and unpredictable, he designed and built a Gothic castle in which he lived and wrote. His environment inspired mysterious stories of romance and intrigue, which led to his title: the father of the Gothic novel. His writing influenced Scott, Byron, Keats, and Coleridge. His insightful and voluminous letters and correspondence give us the clearest picture we have of the social and political life of England's eighteenth century.

Hugh Honour, in his book *Writers and Their Work*, called Walpole "one of the most delightful characters who ever put pen to paper. He knew everyone worth knowing in his elegant age. He had a substantial passion for antiquities, architecture, printing, letter-writing—everything that could enhance the pleasures of life."[11]

You and I may have little in common with this man who was born into wealth and position in such a different time, but he had a freshness that we

> Rather than complacency and laziness, Walpole seemed to derive productivity and widespread interests from his privilege.

can all admire. Knowing a little about his nature is helpful in understanding the word he coined.

British historian Thomas Macaulay said "Walpole rejected, with gay abandon, whatever appeared dull, while retaining only what was in itself amusing or could be made so by the artifice of his diction." Contemporary biographer James Boswell spoke of "Harry's constitutional tranquility or affection of it." Gilly Williams, who knew him from boyhood, said, "I can figure no being happier than Harry." Seventeenth-century novelist William Thackeray, who, like many, felt that Walpole's correspondence was his greatest legacy and contribution, said, "Nothing can be more charming than Horace's letters. Fiddles sing all through them: wax lights, fine dresses, fine jokes, fine plates glitter and sparkle. There never was such a brilliant, jiggling, smirking Vanity Fair as that through which he leads us."[12]

What was it about Walpole that gave him his tranquility, his happiness, his gift of seeing life as a graphic, sparkling, exciting adventure? Was it an attitude—an attitude he already had and for which he found a name when he read the fable of the three princes?

As interesting as the descriptions of Walpole by friends might be, his own words and self-description carry even more insight:

"I have papers to sort; I have letters and books to write; I have my prints to paste, my house to build, and everything in the world to tell posterity—how am I to find time for all this?"

"I love to communicate my satisfactions. My melancholy I generally shut up in my own breast."

"This world is a comedy to those that think, and a tragedy to those that feel."

"In short, the true definition of me is that I am a dancing senator—not that I do dance, or do anything by being a senator; but I go to balls and to the House of Commons—to look on, and you will believe me when I tell you that I really think the former is the more serious occupation of the two: at least the performers are more in earnest."

"What should we gain by triumph [over the colonists]? Would America laid waste, deluged with blood, plundered and enslaved replace America flourishing, rich, and free?"[13]

This man, then, who seemed interested in everything, who loved fun and spontaneity; who was open and candid about his own feelings and weaknesses; who was part cynic, part political critic, part romanticist; and who was always trying to discover what was inside himself as well as out in the world around him—this man coined the word *serendipity*. The concept of happy accidents and good things discovered through awareness and sagacity appealed to him because so much interested him and because life held such adventure and intrigue for him.

Perhaps the most revealing of all Walpole's self-insights was the occasion when he tried to see himself through the eyes of one Reverend Mr. Steward, a fellow guest at the country home of the Earl of Hartford.

Strolling about the house, he saw me first sitting on the pavement of the lumber room with Louis, all over cobwebs and dirt and mortar; then found me in his own room on a ladder writing on a picture; and half an hour afterwards lying on the grass in the court with the dogs and the children, in my slippers and without my hat. He had some doubt whether I was the painter or the workman from the factory or the tutor for the family's children; but you would have died at his surprise when he saw me walk into dinner and sit by Lady Hartford. Lord Lyttelton was there and the conversation turned to literature. Finding me not quite ignorant added to the Reverend's wonder; but when he saw me go to romps and jumping with the two boys, he could stand it no longer and begged to know who and what sort of man I really was, for he had never met with anything of the kind.[14]

MY TRANSLATION

It appears that Walpole cultivated an attitude of awareness, spontaneity, and joy; and that he relished the unexpected, the happy discoveries and surprises of life. Perhaps he found slight frustration in the fact that there was no word to describe the attitude or quality that he most valued.

Then he came upon *The Three Princes of Serendip*. In the story, he found a clear expression of his attitude and, in the title, he found the root for a new word.

The Three Princes of Serendip is the tale of three princes who go out into the world to seek their fortunes and gain experience. While none find fortune, each finds something better. One finds love, one loyalty, and one great service; all find relationships and causes of importance and joy. They find these unexpected things (things that are better than what they were seeking) because of their awareness, their sensitivity, and their sagacity. They notice things that others miss. They are interested in things around them, and thus they find opportunities and friendships and other joys that less aware and less sensitive people do not see.

Walpole fell in love with the fable and essentially said: We don't have a word in our English language that expresses the phenomenon of people looking for one thing, but finding something better than that which they were seeking because of their awareness and sensitivity.

I suppose he thought: I'm an author; I will make up a new word to express this delightful concept. Since it comes from *The Three Princes of Serendip*, I will call it *serendipity*.

Once I learned of the ancient Persian fable that led Walpole to coin the word serendipity, *I wanted to read a copy for myself. Finding a copy was not easy, particularly one that was translated into English. I finally learned that one existed in the ancient collections annex to the Reading Room of the British Museum in London. I flew to England, and when I got to the Museum I spent the first couple of hours marveling at the beauty and majesty of perhaps the largest and most beautiful reading room in the world. I had requested to read the old volume of* The Three Princes *and loved how protective the staff was of the ancient and irreplaceable copies.*

I was not allowed to touch it. A young man with white gloves carried the book in, sat across from me at a reading table, opened the book, and turned the pages when I nodded. I touched the book only with my eyes. But the book touched my heart and my imagination. Not allowed to copy the story, I wrote down as much of it as I

could remember and recreated the story in my earlier book, Spiritual Serendipity.

The story, a fable in the truest sense, beautifully illustrates where peoples' lives can go when they learn to be deeply observant and in tune and when they are willing to subjugate their own goals and strategies to the new paths and possibilities that their awareness reveals.

CHAPTER 3

———

WHAT THE WORD
CAN MEAN TODAY

N   ow that we know a little about serendipity's past, it is time to move
     to the present. What is serendipity today? How does it work now?
     All good explanations involve definitions of terms and stories or
experiences to illustrate. So we will begin there and then move to some practical suggestions on how to gain the quality and how to use it.

Let's start with the kind of serendipity that is both generated and received
by the mind and by the five senses that the mind commands. I call this the
mindset of serendipity.

DEFINITIONS OF TERMS

(THE WORD, AND THE WORDS THAT DEFINE THE WORD)

Serendipity, says a current *Webster's* dictionary, is: "The making of pleasant
discoveries by accident, the knack of doing this."

Walpole would not have been completely satisfied with *Webster's* definition. After reading *The Three Princes*, he wanted a word that meant more than luck or accident. He wanted a word that celebrated life's sometimes happy unpredictability, but he also wanted a word that recognized the fact that luck comes most frequently to those who are aware, concerned, and wise.

> *Serendipity* was defined by Walpole as "that quality of mind which, through sagacity and good fortune, allows one to frequently discover something good while seeking something else."[15]

Serendipitous is the adjectival form. A serendipitous experience is one of unexpected happy discovery, and a serendipitous person is one who makes such discoveries frequently.

Sagacity, *Webster* says, is "wisdom in one's understanding and judgment of things; awareness and insight springing both from education and from alertness." Sagacity, then, requires us to be both informed and aware. It asks us to be alert, sensitive, and empathetic. Just as it has been said that luck favors the prepared, it could be said that serendipity favors the sagacious or the informed and *aware*.

Sensual awareness can be defined as alertness and effective use of the five senses. Each of our senses can be developed—fine-tuned—so they present us with more beauty as well as more information, more opportunities and insight, as well as more data. When we concentrate only on the task at hand, on the schedule, routine, or plan of the day, we are like the plow horse wearing blinders who sees only the straight furrow ahead of him. But when we focus on what is happening as well as what we are doing—and on what is around us and in us—we begin to be as aware of the feelings in our hearts as we are of the plans in our *minds*.

Mental awareness refers to both our education and our insights—our accumulated understanding and perspectives as well as our alertness and vigilance. It refers to our ability to be in the world and aware of the world in the most positive sense.

Good fortune, says *Webster*, is "luck; good things that happen without work or effort."

Again, Walpole wouldn't have been entirely happy with *Webster*. Walpole thought that serendipity could be obtained in greater frequency by developing both sagacity and good fortune.

Good fortune, in his mind, was an attitude of faith and optimism—an attitude allowing one to see the bright, opportunistic side of unexpected occurrences—a love and an appreciation for surprises rather than a resentment of them. Indeed, it is possible to expect the unexpected, to admit that life is unpredictable and that we control only a very small number of the variables, and then to decide to look for the positive interpretation or bright side of everything that happens. This, in Walpole's mind, would constitute the attitude of good fortune.

Goals can best be defined as mental pictures of things as we want them to be. Goals are an essential part of serendipity. The third requirement set forth by Walpole, after sagacity and good fortune, was to be seeking something. Serendipity happens when we discover something good "while seeking something else." It is when we couple awareness and sagacity with purpose and goals that we create the atmosphere and attitudes within which serendipity can flourish. While serendipity is *helped* by goals and direction, it is *hindered* by heavy, overstructured plans and highly detailed lists and schedules that absorb all of our awareness, sucking us away from the opportunities and surprises of the *present*.

Quality of life refers to the joy and fulfillment-level of our everyday living. It does not result from material possessions or external life style. Quality of life results from a quality of the temperament and of the soul which this book calls serendipity.

Bridge reflects the idea that serendipity is a bridge. The metaphor applies in many ways. The first application is that serendipity is a bridge between structure and spontaneity, between discipline and flexibility, between expected and unexpected, between plans and surprises, and between the forced and the fun.

———

As we put this all together we understand that Serendipity
is not a compromise or a midpoint between
structure and spontaneity.
It is a frame of mind that lets a person have more of both
than he could have of either.

Setting goals, with an accompanying determination
to stay flexible and
to keep *looking* for something better
reveals short cuts to the goals one has set
as often as it reveals better goals.

The *sources* as well as the benefits
of serendipity
are physical, mental, social, and emotional.

Physical serendipity involves intense use
of the five senses
and yields greater beauty observed,
adventure,
and the registration of more pleasure and joy, through
what eyes see, ears hear, senses sense.

Mental serendipity trains both the brain's hemispheres
to gather and to value knowledge
and results in understanding,
joyous openings of truth and insight,
and, eventually, real wisdom.

Social serendipity makes us see all people as interesting,
helps us watch for chance meetings, chances to learn,
chances to give,

and puts into our hands the joystick of friends everywhere—
even in places we've never been.

Emotional serendipity
lets us become fascinated with (rather than resentful of)
our own moods.
It is easy to enjoy excitement or delight or peace, but let us also
observe our depression, pensiveness, even our fear,
and find within them insight and depth.

In all cases, serendipity involves a certain combination
of awareness, observation, acceptance, and optimism
that lets us find the best in
whoever we are with,
whatever is going on,
wherever we are,
whenever we are living, and
however we are feeling.
In all cases we are
Finding and flowing
Instead of forcing and fighting.

———

Scientists, explorers, and inventors tell us that their discoveries come in one of two ways: solitary periods of private, penetrating, almost painful thought, or bursts of insight that come not out of analysis but out of observation or out of incidental conversation—or out of nowhere.

It is the same with our discoveries about ourselves and life. They come to us either through deep, free thought, or through observation and awareness. Each is undermined by trying to control everything, by frantic activity, and by excessive technology and screentime.

As a society, we are more and more aware of the challenge of personal balance and of doing well in our work without sacrificing our families or our personal interests. We keep getting offered the same old tired "cures" of

positive mental attitude and time management. Many people carry both to excess. Positive mental attitude starts to mean controlling everything and time management starts to mean making longer and longer lists and trying to do more and more things.

Serendipity is an alternative attitude, a rescuer. It involves being positive and having goals, but it also involves flexibility, spontaneity, sensitivity, and the relish of surprise.

———

THE SOURCE

(You)
Whence cometh serendipity?
From ourselves!
It is a quality and a gift
that can be given only by ourselves
and only to ourselves.
We give it by teaching ourselves to *notice* and *think,*
to look for beauty, ideas, relationships—
to relish the unexpected,
to welcome surprises as opportunities,
even if they delay or alter (and sometimes replace)
the goals we have thoughtfully set and diligently pursued.

Serendipity is a translucent, rose-colored umbrella
that overarches—
our physical, mental, social, and emotional lives,
making them dynamic, and allowing each part of us
to see.

Serendipity is an infrared, wide-angle lens that lets us
See more
and see each part clear and light.

Where cometh serendipity?
It is a seeing, a light, even in darkness
From you.

—

THE PROCESS

The development of serendipity is not merely a mental process, like learning a new memory technique, or a physical process, like muscle conditioning. Rather, it is the adopting of an attitude of thoughtfulness and watchfulness that physically slows us up, emotionally calms us down, socially opens us out, and mentally turns us in.

One way to see how the right amount of planning or seeking combined with sagacity can work in real life is to make a two-sided list. If you're a list-maker, make your list (or write your schedule) on the left side of your page. Draw a line down the center and leave the right side blank to jot down the day's serendipity after it happens (a new acquaintance, a fresh idea, a child's question, an unexpected opportunity, a friend's need, a chance meeting, a beautiful sunset).

For fun, at the end of the week, look back on the lefts and rights of your days and discover that what just happened on the unknown right is often more valuable than what you planned on the known left.

After my initial discovery of the idea of serendipity, I continued to use a rather bulky and detailed scheduling book. Then one day it occurred to me that too much detail in planning was making me less receptive to the kind of awareness and sagacity I was seeking. About that time, I made the following observations in my journal:

> Too much planning can make the actual experience of living almost anticlimactic. (There may be times for reading the script, but it's never as exciting as ad-libbing.)

Too much thinking about something removes us from it—we become observers, analysts, spectators, or critics rather than participants.

If we can approach life more as an experience that contains vast variety and infinite potential for surprise we will find ourselves dealing less with success and failure and more with progress and growth.

If we have to think about every detail of our lives, we ought to think about them after they have been lived (when we can learn from experience) not before and during (when the very thought may intercept or alter the experience).

Approaching life as an experience makes us, moment-to-moment, more aware of what is happening and of what we are feeling—and less aware of what we plan to have happen or wish had happened. Thus, we see the opportunities we could never have planned and realize far more serendipity that we otherwise could.

Goals can coexist with experience—they can shine like beacons and allow us to see our experiences more clearly in their order and light.

Since the time that I made these observations, I have tried to do what I call *picturing* instead of planning. I still write down my goals, and I write down what I think I might have to do to reach them, but in much more general terms than before.

I use the left side of my planning page to keep track of appointments and schedules, but I am committed to right-side serendipity and to regular sessions to reevaluate where I am going and what alternative routes there may be to get there. One day, in my journal, I tried to reduce my new approach to a two-line motto:

Be strong and fixed on the destination,
but creative and flexible on the route.

SERENDIPITY IN SHORT

Walpole, whether he knew it or not, told us *how* to get serendipity right in his definition of the word. "The ability," he said "through sagacity and good fortune to find something good while looking for something else."

Three requirements:

1. *Sagacity*: notice, watch, observe, be aware, learn, refuse to wear the blinders of obsession or self-consciousness.

2. The attitude of *good fortune*: see changes as opportunities, surprises as excitement, disappointments with silver linings.

3. Thoughtful *goals*: set and list objectives and pursue them until something else (better) is discovered.

CHAPTER 4

——

THE REALM
OF SPIRITUAL
SERENDIPITY

Y ou know by now that this book is not shying away from spiritual constructs and terminology. This is justified partly by polls mentioned earlier that reveal that 75 percent of Americans express belief in a higher power and more than 90 percent call themselves spiritual.[16]

But the bigger justification for the spiritual perspective is that it is the only way of explaining some of the most beautiful things that happen in our lives and in our minds. Because spiritual feelings and identity can be so different in each of us, some effort has been made to avoid the use of specific religious terminology and choose words like "higher intelligence" or "the divine" rather than constantly saying "God" and raising questions about which God or whose God.

So, please, when the terms "God" or "higher power" are used, interpret them into your own lexicon of belief, and if a general sense of spirituality

works better for you than specific beliefs about a god, move forward and read on within your own spiritual paradigm. The purpose of this book is not to define or write of God, but to encourage you to stay open and accepting of the beyond-our-senses insights, epiphanies, and guidance that come to us from sources that can best be termed *spiritual*. And if I quote from the Bible or from Buddha or from *Beowulf*, focus on the power of what the quote says, not on your literal belief in the history or source of the quote.

Prose and logic and proof and science have their place in the world, but it is often not in that place that we understand the power and subtly of our attitudes, of our paradigms, and of how we know and feel certain things. For these, we need the spiritual perspective and the poetic interpretation. G. K. Chesterton said it well:

"Poetry is sane because it floats easily in an infinite sea; reason seeks to cross the infinite sea, and so make it finite. The result is mental exhaustion. To . . . understanding everything is a strain . . . the poet only asks to get his head into the heavens. It is the logician who seeks to get the heavens into his head. And it is his head that splits."[17]

Even though it is best understood and applied after understanding and learning to apply serendipity with our basic five senses, *spiritual* serendipity is something completely different—a separate and higher form—different not only in degree but in kind—a heartset rather than a mindset.

With a mindset of serendipity, our awareness comes through perceptions of our senses and through the light of education, great books, great minds, and our own feelings. With a heartset of spiritual serendipity, our awareness comes through the perception of our spirit and, for some, the light of scripture and prophets. The nudges and impressions we experience come from God, nature, the universe.

Just as the quality itself is higher, so is the method and process of pursuit higher (and harder). But it is worth all the effort we can give, because the rewards of spiritual serendipity, simply put, are light and understanding, guidance and direction, happiness and joy.

DEFINITIONS OF TERMS

(THE WORDS THAT DEFINE A SPIRITUAL QUALITY)

Spiritual serendipity: That quality or gift which, through sagacity of both senses and spirit, and through grace, allows one to seek and receive guidance, inspiration, confirmation, and knowledge relative to one's purpose, family, opportunities for service, and day-to-day activities.

Gift: While serendipity is a gift from ourselves, spiritual serendipity is a gift from God. Since it relies on powers and perceptions beyond our own, it can be given only by a higher power. Still, it is *we* who determine whether we obtain the gift, because it is freely given to all who desire it and do what it requires.

Sixth Sense: Most sensitive individuals recognize that the five senses are not their only source of knowledge or information. We can tune into nudges, impressions, and insights (sometimes called inspiration). Our sixth sense consists of the feelings of our inner spirits or our souls.

I remember a discussion with a stranger on an airplane about what is most real. He was a skeptic who took the attitude "I'll believe it if I can see it." Just for the sake of argument and to make the flight time go faster, I asked him if he was married and if he loved his wife. When he said "Yes" and "Yes," I asked him if he could see that love. He said, "No, but I feel it." And that made my point.

Nudges: Impressions that come to our minds via our spirits.

Tuning In: Like a faint radio signal, nudges can be tuned in and amplified until they become clear and spiritually audible.

Bridge II: While serendipity is a bridge between our structured selves and spontaneous selves, spiritual serendipity is a bridge between *our* goals and purpose, and God's will for us or life's purpose. It is also a bridge between

the inspiration we receive during meditation, prayer, or planning and the nudges that come later—on the spur of the moment.

Foreordination: A more conditional way of saying destiny. Do you ever feel like you have a very specific purpose, something you just have to do, whether in terms of what you need to do on a particular day or before you grow old? The idea of foreordination is that we each have certain capacities or gifts and we are born to accomplish particular things while here on earth. True fulfillment comes from finding and fulfilling one's foreordination or destiny.

Ask: We are given the opportunity to ask for personal guidance. Some ask through meditation or prayer, others ask with a simple question in their heart as they take a walk or go through their day. There is no wrong way to seek guidance.

> *I had an acquaintance who was partial to (and gifted in) statistics and mathematics. He took delight in asking me questions he knew I couldn't answer. One day he said, "What do you think is the most frequently repeated admonition in all of scripture?" I guessed that it was something to do with love. "No," he said. "The most frequent admonition is to ask."*
>
> *He was referring specifically to the Holy Bible, but said that the same admonition occurs frequently in the scriptures of all religions. I've thought about that a great deal. Why would it be such a recurrent theme? Why is God so insistent that we ask, that we knock—and so consistent in promising us that answers will follow?*

I think the closest I come to understanding this principle is in my role as a father. I want my children to be individuals, to be independent and free, but I also have a lot of advice I want to give them; I know I'll still feel that way no matter how old they are and how far away from me they might live. If they ask, I'll be able to give help and counsel that won't undermine their independence or their freedom. If they ask, it will be their initiative, not mine.

To me, a God, who allows us to make our own choices and learn at our pace, remains a loving spiritual guide. Just like any parent, he cares for us and desires to give to us. But to give without invitation would constitute interference. No wonder, then, that we are told so often to ask!

Inspiration: A higher power's communication with humanity. It comes sometimes in the form of confirmation and answers to our requests—as guidance as we meditate, pray, and seek for answers to our life questions. It comes at other times in quick nudges and impressions—tiny, soft, fleeting suggestions to our spirits.

Spirit: Two meanings: our own spirits or souls, the part of each of us, which I will call spirit with a lower case *s*; and God's Spirit, the Holy Spirit, or Spiritual power of the Universe. This Spirit, which can influence and enlighten each of us, I will refer to with a capital *S*.

A GUIDED LIFE

As with a mindset of serendipity, spiritual serendipity cannot be completely defined with words, because, more than a word, it is a feeling. Words are useful only if they generate some image or glimpse of the feeling. Spiritual serendipity is the soft, sweet submission of spirit, a conscious dependency on God. To a Christian, it is a decision to "rely alone upon the merits of Christ." To a spiritualist it has to do with the connection between all things. To a Hindu, it might reference other past or future lives. To a Muslim, it is the acceptance of Allah.

It is the rigorous realization that when it comes to long-range planning, life is too complex for our own calculations—thus the goal of a guided life, guided by a higher, more comprehensive source.

—

Spiritual serendipity is sunshine,
which lights and reveals
what would otherwise be dark and unnoticed.
It is the excitement and intrigue of a great game
in which we ask questions and make requests
and then try to summon the sensitivity necessary

to recognize the answers,
which come sometimes
with much softness and subtlety.

———

Because the spirit gives life and light to the body, spiritual serendipity trans-
mits to and affects our every part. A religious leader named Parley Pratt, nearly
two centuries ago, spoke of a force which could

> ... adapt itself to all our organs or attributes ... It quickens all the intel-
> lectual faculties; increases, enlarges, expands, and purifies all the natural
> passions and affections. It inspires, develops, cultivates, and matures all
> the fine-toned sympathies, joys, tastes, kindred feelings, and affections
> of our nature. It inspires virtue, kindness, goodness, tenderness, gentle-
> ness, and charity. It develops beauty of person, form, and features. It
> tends to health, vigor, animation, and social feeling. It invigorates all the
> faculties of the physical and intellectual man. It strengthens and gives
> tone to the nerves ... it is ... joy to the heart, light to the eyes, music to
> the ears, and life to the whole being.[18]

Pratt also compared the spirit with electricity, explaining how it could warm
and light those who, as pure conductors, let it enter them. This metaphor of
electricity, dramatic in the mid-nineteenth century, is perhaps even more profound now that electricity is everywhere present and always at our disposal.

The spirit of God, into which we can "plug" ourselves, is always there and
always here. The circuitry is complete. No new line ever has to be jerry-rigged
to answer our asking or meet our needs. We simply must understand how to
plug in. When we do, we and the world around us are transformed.

> We once had an old wheat grinder that could be operated either electri-
> cally or manually with a big iron hand crank. With a thought toward
> building the family arm muscles, I insisted that we grind by people-
> power. One evening, several of the children and I were out in the

breezeway of our home where we kept the grinder taking turns at the handle. That night, because time was short and I had to get to a meeting, we finally plugged in the grinder. I watched the children's eyes as they watched the transformation. The hum and steady friction of the stone wheels warmed the whole machine and it seemed to glow with incredible strength and efficiency. Power, warmth, energy, peace. The grinder could do more in five minutes with electricity than we could make it do in an hour. It worked with ease, softly, calmly. The power was there all the time, waiting. We only needed to plug it in.

———

The power of God's spirit, transmittable to ours,
is so vast.
And its vastness alone, like a slow, sweeping river
turning a water-wheel generator,
makes it peaceful and calm, easy while strong.

We plug in with a three-prong plug of awareness:
First, a prong of sensual awareness
that reveals opportunity, need, and deep reality to us
through our five senses.
Second, a prong of spiritual awareness,
a knowing both of our own spiritual selves and
of a higher spirit,
together with an in-tuneness that pulls us to ask.
Third, a prong of attitudinal awareness
that allows us to expect discoveries of interest and joy;
to savor the surprises of sense and spirit.
It is the attitude herein called spiritual serendipity,
adopted into our souls,
which calms us, opens our vision,
and sweeps us into the currents of light.

———

We pursue spiritual serendipity, then, by developing awareness through the senses, through the spirit, and through an attitude that values, cultivates, and interconnects the two. It could be well argued that the accumulation of additional awareness is synonymous with progress . . . and that the difference between God and humanity, vast as it is, is in part a difference in awareness.

We may be ready now for a clearer, simpler definition of spiritual serendipity: It is the aware, submissive, and sensitive condition of our spirits which makes them susceptible to the calm, the light, the peace, and the power of The Spirit.

JAMES ON SERENDIPITY

One of the most fascinating (though little quoted and little understood) verses in the New Testament comes from the fourth chapter of James, verses 13–15:

> *Go to now ye that say: today or tomorrow we will go into such a city and continue there a year and buy and sell and get gain . . . Ye know not what shall be on the morrow . . . Your life . . . is even a vapor.*

One remarkable thing about these verses is the current sound of their terminology. With minor adjustments, they seem to translate into blunt criticisms of the pseudo-positive attitude, goal-setting salesmanship, and high-achievement mentality of today. It could almost read:

> *Watch out when you say things like, "our plan calls for us to go into such and such a city tomorrow and over a year's time we will meet the sales quota and accomplish our business plan." The fact is that you can't plan or control very much of what will happen in the future. There are so many factors involved and you are not of that much consequence.*

The advice that follows within that scripture is also as current and as important today as it was then:

For today ye ought to say "if the Lord will, we shall live, and do this or that."

Perhaps only God knows enough about our future to be able to tell us what we should do and who we should be.

Was James telling us not to set goals or make plans? Or was he just reminding us of how little we really control?

Unexpected, impossible to anticipate situations, events, occurrences (and also feelings, nudges, and impressions) enter our lives almost every day. We really don't know what the morrow will hold. The question is not whether we can anticipate, predict, and plan everything. We can't!

The question is whether we will try to avoid, ignore, or push aside things not of our making, things which don't quite fit with our plans . . . or will we relish them, embrace them, look for the serendipity in them? Will we accept and love and look for the feelings of the spirit which come as inner suggestions, and subtle, unexpected answers to the questions of our hearts and prayers?

So, back to the question, is James telling us we are unwise to set goals and make plans? Is life a card game with results based mainly on the luck of the draw? Or a chess game where we are the pawns moved only by God's will?

No. No. And no.

But life might well be thought of as a game of *ask and answer*. We ask for insight and direction to know our purpose or what we should do, and God, spirit, nature answers—always—but not always in the way or at the time or the place we expect. The answers may come quickly and directly to us as we ask and analyze, ponder and plan; or they may come later in unexpected formats at unexpected moments.

These answers are missed by those with too rigid plans because it is outside of their own ideas.

These answers are also missed by those without any goals or plans, because they have not thought enough to be able to recognize the answers when they come.

THE GAME OF "ASK AND ANSWER"

In this game, the wise player connects
the answers that come with the goals he has set and the
questions she has asked.

The game is won by thinking hard about the right goals
and the right questions
and then finding (or recognizing when they faintly appear)
the right answers.

So . . . ask and answer is a difficult game
but an uncommonly rewarding one.
And the winners are the thinkers, the askers,
and the listeners.

Think of it for a moment in terms of realms:
One in which people float, sometimes passive,
sometimes resentful,
letting the world push, mold, shove, and shape them
as it will,
following the course of least resistance . . .
going nowhere, slowly.

There is another realm
where people do their best to take control
of themselves and their destinies . . .
shaping events, setting goals, making things happen;
drawing a blueprint and then building it.

There is a third realm
It involves:
Thoughtfully setting goals
asking and striving to have inspiration to find and fulfill our purpose.
(God gives us a light even as we pray.)

Watching for answers, further light and knowledge,
nudges that make our destiny, our foreordination, or purpose clearer
and then accepting, acting,
and changing our goals to fit the clearer view.

———

The beauty of having faith to ask and to follow shine through the well-known verse that was quoted by King George VI in his Christmas Day broadcast in the dark, war-filled days of 1939.

I said to the man who stood at the Gate of the Year,
"Give me light that I may tread safely into the unknown."
And he replied, "Go out into the darkness, and put your hand into the
hand of God.
That shall be to you better than light, and safer than a known way."[19]

If *notice and think* are the keys to serendipity, then the two-word methodology for spiritual serendipity is *watch and pray*. Answers come sometimes as we pray or meditate, sometimes later as we watch.

Most people let life's currents make their decisions for them. This fact
started to become clear to me as a university student. A man much
wiser than I asked me why I was majoring in a certain subject. I re-
plied that it was because my uncle had that profession. He said, "So
what, why do you want to have the same job?" I said, "Because I like
my uncle."
He then told me that most of the world makes decisions that way.
We drift into choices because someone else has already made them;
we take a path because it is the most known and least threatening to
us at the time.

We forget about things like deep personal analysis and prayer and guidance until life delivers us a dire dilemma or a clear crisis. Without these prompts, we just float with the current in pleasant waters, thinking little

about where we're going. Before long we find ourselves believing that the main goal is to avoid the rapids (not understanding that those rapids may be the only exciting part of the trip).

How many of the answers come us as we pray and meditate and how many come as we watch is up to divine wisdom.

A grad school friend of mine became so concerned about knowing what to do with his life and with knowing God's will and understanding his destiny that he dropped out of classes (and out of sight) for several days to fast and pray about it. He said he got some feelings and some glimpses, but mostly he got this answer: Keep working and keep asking; I'll tell you more in my own way, in my own time, when you are ready to understand more.

So, he went on—much like the locomotive engineer who was asked "How do you drive this massive train at eighty miles an hour in the dead of night when your headlight only lights the track for one hundred yards?" "I have found," the engineer said, "that when I reach the end of that hundred yards, I see clearly the next hundred yards."

THE EXQUISITE TIMING OF DIVINE GUIDANCE

Most guidance comes at one of two times: as we pray (and plan and ponder and struggle to understand) or as we watch (and are sagacious and sensitive and open to answers in surprises and subtle forms). This higher realm of guidance involves a whole new approach to life, an approach where we set long- and short-range goals, but watch and pray for the added insight and the expanded opportunity that may lift those goals to higher and happier and healthier levels.

It is an approach that requires frequent reevaluation, meditation, and prayer. It is an approach available to those who believe in a God or spirituality which can and will give light. It requires an understanding that we possess far too little knowledge, far too narrow an understanding to adequately guide ourselves.

All who believe in these two things (God's love and our own inadequacy) have the reason for wanting and the perspective required for gaining spiritual serendipity.

THE SOURCE OF SPIRITUAL SERENDIPITY (AND SOME SPIRITUAL ALGEBRA)

We have defined spiritual serendipity as a feeling, a quality, an attitude, a condition of *our* spirit (calm, aware, peaceful, still, sure) that makes us more receptive to God's Spirit and joy. So, the Spirit is not only the *source* of that feeling or condition, but the *result* of it . . . right?

If S = spiritual serendipity and G = God's Spirit,

Then S brings G. Or, in math language, If S, then G . . . right?

Actually, that's not it. Let's put in a missing piece and turn it around.

The answers and insights we are looking for (call them A) are often already here—around us and inside us. Serendipity of our spirits lets us see them, find them, feel them. And it is the Spirit that gives this serendipity to our spirits.

So: G brings S which reveals A!

God's Spirit brings spiritual serendipity which reveals answers and insights. The Spirit *is* the source of spiritual serendipity.

Let us return to Parley Pratt's discussion of the spirit and of our own attributes. He said that we "possess every organ, attribute, sense, sympathy, and affection that is possessed by God Himself. But these are possessed by man in a rudimental state . . . these attributes are in embryo . . . they resemble a bud . . . which gradually develops into bloom."[20]

Pratt makes it clear that the force that awakens all these faculties, that enlarges, expands, our natural mind is the Spirit. The Spirit is the source of the serendipity of our spirits.

Perhaps there are other sources which can enlighten and clarify our minds. Deep meditation brings a certain stillness and serendipity, making one open to unexpected discoveries about self and life. And a slow, measurable alpha

state brain wave pattern, which brightens creativity and sharpens insight, can be obtained through techniques ranging from breathing disciplines to hypnosis.

But the Spirit is the complete source, the reliable source.

Once while we were living in England, I set out one day during a school vacation to take my three teenage daughters on a short trip to France. We had a list of things we wanted to see and do, and I had in mind a couple of topics I wanted to discuss with the girls in the privacy of our trip. We drove all the way to Dover on England's south coast, lined up for the ferry and got all the way to the passport checkpoint, twenty feet from the ferry ramp, only to discover, under a new ruling by the French government, we had to have visas.

Seeing the girls' disappointment, I said a silent prayer for serendipity. The gloom of "we've wasted our vacation" soon gave way to youthful optimism and to the notion of freedom and discovery. We turned around and set out along the south coast of England. Our new goal was now to make discoveries. In an obscure antique store in Folkstone we found a wonderful bargain on the type of dining room table we had dreamed of. In an Indian tandoori restaurant, we discovered a cuisine totally new to the girls and made friends with two British couples who told us about the quaint Wellington Hotel. In Tunbridge Wells we found the remarkable old Wellington Hotel and stayed overnight in a wonderful Victorian room.

Later, on a long, dark stretch of road something one of the girls said started a spontaneous, free discussion of marriage relationships, and I had the opportunity to discuss exactly the points that I had hoped to bring up in France.

The next day, on a train, we got acquainted with a Scottish man and his two small children who became our new friends. The whole two days were filled with happy surprises. Chances to teach, chances to form and deepen relationships, and serendipitous discoveries occurred on many levels.

We didn't get to France, but we got to a better place in our relationships.

When we ask for the Spirit to guide our growth, to give us wings of thoughtful awareness, we develop the heartset and connect ourselves to the source-current of spiritual serendipity.

—

TWO WAYS TO INCREASE YOUR INCIDENTS OF SERENDIPITY

There are two ways to obtain the guidance that can lead to more of spiritually serendipitous experiences. As mentioned earlier, one way is to *watch* and the other way is to *pray* or meditate. Here are four approaches for each.

PRAYING OR MEDITATING FOR GUIDANCE: FOUR SUGGESTIONS FOR DEVELOPMENT OF THE ART

1.

HOLD REGULAR WEEKLY SESSIONS AND SET GOALS WITHOUT PLANS

Set aside an hour of solitude each week to review the directions and goals of your life through quiet thought and prayer.

Use spiritual tools from the broad and general to the specific and personal—anything from scriptures and sermons to podcasts and Ted Talks, to your own notes, diary entries, and answers you have felt as you pray or even on your morning commute. You are a ship with your own internal compass and guidance systems, but you can also get bearings from the heavens.

Project in writing where you want to be and what you want to happen in your family, in your work, in your personal life five years from now. Then thoughtfully, prayerfully, enhance and adjust your plan according to your impressions and answers to prayers—adjust and refine your goals from week to week in this prayerful weekly session.

Reflect and ponder on how you will reach these goals. With long-range goals, be content with broad brush strokes and conceptual images. Stop short of the detailed, complex plans that assume you know more than you really do as this can block the way of both inspiration and discovery.

God often confirms the "what" and helps us with our "why" as we pray. Then, if we are spiritually sagacious, the spirit refines and adjusts the "where," "when," and "how" (and sometimes even adds to the "what") as we watch.

2.

ASK

We have already established asking as the most repeated admonition of scripture and as the key that unlocks blessings and guidance without violation of our agency. Because of its power, we must be careful in our asking. When asking is thoughtful, and when it follows unselfish thanking, asking polishes us and pleases God. Prayer becomes sweet and delicious and hard to conclude.

Good askers are good listeners; they are willing to watch and wait.

Prayer sometimes yields inspiration about what we can do to answer our question or meet our needs. Other times prayer is not the source of an answer or the channel by which we are guided to do something; rather, it *is* the answer and brings about the change by itself without directing us to do anything.

Sometimes prayer points us toward power.

Sometimes it *is* the power.

There are at least three very different types of prayer in which guidance is sought:

- Prayer for change wrought by God

This is where we ask a higher power to bring to pass things far beyond our own capacity or power.

- Prayer for light

This is where we seek a clear mind, insight, wisdom, true impressions, and direction toward correct decisions and our purpose . . . so that we can decide what to do and then do it.

- Prayer for confirmation

This comes after we have made a decision and are asking if our decision aligns with God's will for us.

This third prayer deserves further discussion and is the third way to develop the art of prayer.

3.

SEEK CONFIRMATION

Acknowledging the short limits of our understanding, we seek confirmation—the still, sure nod that says "yes" to our studied-out goals and decisions. At this level, our prayers are true/false rather than multiple choice. We can hope to feel either a spiritual, calm knowing—an answer of "yes"—or a stupor of thought or the confusion that indicates our decision is not the best one we could make.

Confirmation, once received, is confidence and support in hard times and freedom from the plague of second-guessing ourselves.

I learned a lot once by failing to do this. I had been offered a presidential appointment to direct a once-a-decade White House Conference. It dealt with a worthy subject (children and parents), it was a clear opportunity, and it would allow us to spend a year in Washington. It also seemed to open doors to other contributions we hoped to make. Linda and I discussed it, talked to the children, and became collectively excited about a tentative decision to go. But in prayer the confirmation didn't come. I wanted the assurance of a confirmation, I tried for it, I even tried to imagine that I had felt it. But if you're not sure you've felt it—you haven't. We discussed it again, we couldn't think of any negatives other than the inconvenience of a move back to Washington where we already owned a home, and the need to turn parts of our business over to others for a time. Then we rationalized a little. Maybe it didn't matter that much whether we accepted or declined. Maybe this wasn't a stupor of thought we were getting but rather an "Okay, fine, go ahead if you want to."

We went ahead. It was one of those interesting decisions that wasn't really wrong, but wasn't really right either. It was not the best

choice we could have made. Only a few weeks after our return to Washington, President Reagan was shot and his recovery, coupled with other factors, led him to de-emphasize the conference and re-direct most of its activity to the state level rather than the national level, which I was assigned to direct. We realized that there would have been ways in which we could have had the same experience without giving up as much as we did—I could have chaired the conference rather than directed it. We had made a decision based on limited foresight and realized later that what had come to us in prayer was a confusion of thought, signaling the need to rethink and take a different approach.

A stupor of mind or confusion of thought that comes when we ask for confirmation is a signal to start over. Either the wrong fork has been taken or something has been left out, a piece is missing somewhere. Or perhaps the timing is wrong.

Confusion is the *absence* of the sureness and is both as real and as valuable as the confirmation.

4.

DEVELOP THE ATTITUDE OF "NOTHINGNESS"

G. K. Chesterton said, "It is impossible without humility to enjoy any-thing—even pride." He also said, "If a man would make his world large, he must make himself small." Indeed, we cannot fully appreciate God's greatness or maximize the power and use of faith until we understand (or at least acknowledge) our own nothingness.

*God wants us to know both how unlimited our potential is
and how far we have to go to reach it;
so that we can feel both the familiarity of closeness
and the awe of distance.*

The scholar Neal Maxwell said, "The more we ponder where we stand in relation to Christ the more we realize that we do not stand at all . . . we only kneel."

For Christians, as well as for all believers in a higher power, the attitude of awe is part of the recipe for spiritual serendipity.

WATCHING FOR GUIDANCE: FOUR SUGGESTIONS FOR DEVELOPING THE ART

1.

ADD CALMNESS AND CURIOSITY TO THE ATTITUDE

Having a mindset of serendipity requires sagacity and an attitude of calm, interested watching. Spiritual serendipity requires the addition of a higher and deeper watching through a still, observant soul, and through the inner eye of the spirit. For this realm, we need to develop a heartset wherein we not only try to see the little things, but we try to see them *as answers*.

Once we have asked we must watch for unexpected answers in unexpected places or forms.

Answers are sometimes found in silver linings and other times in the clouds themselves.

Taking off on a business flight one evening we flew west, up into a heavy cloud bank and toward the sunset. The deep gray was haloed by gold and the metaphor of silver linings passed through my mind. We entered the cloud and experienced some bouncing and buffeting. Then we burst through it directly into the yellow

brilliance of the setting sun—high enough now that the sun had come back up.

It's interesting, I thought, that the clouds which often dominate our vision are only vapors . . . while the silver lining is the reality of the sun.

The attitude that spurs spiritual serendipity not only causes us to look for silver linings, but helps us understand that, despite appearances, they are more vast and stronger by far than the clouds in front of them. Both the linings and the clouds are provided by the same source. Ask as though everything depended on God (because it does). Watch as though everything depended on you (because the answer may be right in front of you or right inside of you). When you watch with calmness and curiosity you will see and understand more.

2.

ADD GRATITUDE AND FASTING TO ATTITUDE

Why would gratitude help us to watch?

Because gratitude is awareness of blessings!

The same perceptive inner-sight that reveals gratitude for what has happened also reveals answers and guidance on what is happening.

Thankfulness is perfect training for watchfulness. One who sees the past's blessings sees also the present's answers and the future's opportunities.

In the New Testament, Paul gives us a similar message in Philippians 4:6–7. He says (in my interpretation) that if, instead of being careful and detailed in our own planning, we make our requests known to God, with thanksgiving, we will have the peace of God in heart and mind that gives serendipity to our spirits.

Many years ago, we started a Thanksgiving tradition in our family of listing our blessings. Before we sit down to turkey dinner, we

*make a list on a long roll of paper of every blessing we can think of.
Everyone in the family gets involved and we list everything from "a
free country" to "indoor plumbing." After dinner, we have contests to
see who can read the entire list in the shortest amount of time. Each
time we do it, we realize that gratitude is more than something we
owe to God. It is a beautiful feeling. It is something we should summon and savor as a gift.*

"Gratitude," as I say in another book, "is not merely a path to happiness . .
. Gratitude IS happiness in its most obtainable form."[21]

Fasting, a principle correctly thought of in connection with asking for
blessings and understanding, can also be of great assistance in giving thanks
for blessings.

Fasting sharpens our physical senses and tunes in our spiritual senses,
making us highly susceptible to spiritual serendipity. And intermittent
fasting, which is gaining attention as a weight-loss technique, can be
health-giving to the body as well as the soul.

3.

RECORD AND REMEMBER NUDGES

—

When a nudge or impression touches our spirit
(sometimes just bushing gently across it)
the worst thing we can do is ignore it.
The second worst thing we can do is to forget it.
Impressions often reach clarity only for an instant and then,
Immediately,
begin to fade, dim, and dissipate . . .

Unless we seize them and transfer them
into our conscious mind
where they can be held solid and clear.

—

The first time we moved to England our children were small and everything was an exciting adventure to them. When we returned for our second stay, we had teenagers—who added whole new levels to the concept of homesickness. Just a week after we arrived, and before homesickness began, I was running an errand to the shops with our fifteen-year-old and felt a clear nudge to talk with her about the homesickness that would probably set in after the excitement wore off. It was clear to me for a moment just how to explain certain things—just what to say to prepare her and soften the blow. But we were nearing the shops, so I decided to wait and discuss it later. A half hour later, on the way home, I brought up the concept of homesickness, but the clear insight into how to explain it and prepare her for it was gone. Several days later, when the symptoms had arrived in force, we talked again (I talked; she sobbed) and I was able to explain some of what I should have explained earlier. As I did, I realized how much better it would have been if I had followed the nudge when it first came.

Learn to recognize impressions that come from the spirit and categorize them not with imagination, superstition, or chance, but rather with inspiration and insight.

Focus on nudges and remember them. If possible, act on them immediately. If not, capture them by writing them down. As you write, they will expand and become clearer. Writing can be thought of as the tuning in that makes a faint signal audible and understandable. Once written it will not be forgotten.

4.

USE SPLIT-PAGE PLANNING WITH NUDGE NOTES

When a spiritual impression comes, it may not be something you can do immediately but something you should do at a certain time or someone you should see or something you should say. The best place to make notes on these nudges is on a calendar or in your smartphone, so that you commit yourself to a specific time on a particular day.

Other impressions may come in the form of broader, longer-range ideas that can be implemented over time, or in the form of new insights which have no particular or immediate application but bear remembering.

These longer-range impressions also need to be captured in writing. When they are not written down, they are loose and somehow soluble—they dissolve and disappear.

Both short- and long-range nudges can best be recorded with the same split-page planning mentioned earlier and described in more detail in a coming chapter. Impressions that dictate action can be committed to by an entry on a particular day (schedule on the left-hand side). Broader ideas and insights from the same source can be captured and expanded in the form of notes on the right-hand side.

Whatever kind of datebook or app you use can be turned into a split-page *anti-planner* by the simple addition of a vertical line to divide each day.

Spiritual insights and inspiration can sometimes be like a faint radio signal, but as we tune into it, the signal gets stronger and we hear it more easily.

During your weekly sessions, have a flip-through review of the past week. Pay special attention to any nudge notes on the right-hand side of each day. Think about how they can be implemented in the future.

THE SERMON

This chapter suggests the formula or recipe for calmness, for watching, for sagacity, and for peaceful, thoughtful prayer. But there is a far better statement

of the necessary ingredients of serendipity, far more beautiful, far clearer, elegantly poetic, and filled with perfect images and feelings. The best way you could follow up on these ideas on serendipity is to set it aside this book and read instead from the Bible.

Whether or not you are a Christian or have ever read from the Bible, Jesus's Sermon on the Mount holds a kind of simple but profound wisdom for how to live a good and joyful life.

One way to read the sermon is as an explanation and set of directions of and for serendipity of the spirit. Read and feel some of the messages and see how they point us toward the attitudes this chapter has tried to describe. Jesus's words are in italics.

- *Build your house on a rock—seek treasures in heaven.* Build your life on strong, righteous goals, but once they are set . . .
- *Take less thought for the morrow.* Don't try to plan everything. Be more like the lilies of the field, the birds in the air—spontaneous, sensitive, flexible.
- **The light of the body is the eye.** See and watch and be filled with light. Ye are the light of the world.
- **Ask.** And answers will open. Look for those answers and accept them, even if they come in unexpected ways. Ask, look, and know.
- **Do not anger or lust.** Control the mind and think purely and deeply.
- **Turn your other cheek . . . give your cloak . . . love enemies.** Instead of judging, strive to see and understand.
- **Fast in secret, pray in closet, let not the left hand see what the right hand gives.** Have pure, inner motives.
- *Rejoice.* Even in adversity. Relish and welcome surprises and unexpected turns of all kinds.
- *Don't let salt lose its savor.* Don't let life get boring—keep your freshness and spontaneity.
- *Be perfect* in loving. Develop the perfect attitude of receptivity, acceptance, awareness, and peace. Record

and remember and implement every nudge the Spirit gives.

Perhaps it is through something like spiritual serendipity that *the meek inherit the earth*, and that the *humble in spirit see the Kingdom of God*. I invite you to read the greatest sermon again, directly from its source in Matthew, chapters 5, 6, and 7. Read it as a recipe for spiritual serendipity. Read it and rediscover its peaceful wisdom.

S U M M A R Y

This part of this book ends as it began—with promises. Hopefully we have made a circle which captures the ideas necessary to make the promises feel accessible.

Think for a moment about the applications of spiritual serendipity—about the benefits that come from being watchful and prayerful and using the resulting calm, receptive serendipity in each facet of our lives.

IN OUR WORK

Spiritual serendipity makes us happier in our work by relaxing us, reducing stress; it helps us find adventure in the day-to-day possibilities and opportunity in the small and unexpected.

It lets us stop pushing and forcing and lets us start seeing creative solutions and lateral thinking approaches.

Even if your work is, by nature, very routine, spiritual serendipity will allow you to see and appreciate people and things that make each day more interesting.

As mentioned in side one, I had a professor who preached a mantra that went something like this: "Try never to be surprised. If you are surprised, it shows you're not a very good anticipator or planner and your business

life will be unpredictable and constantly upsetting. Act, don't react, because we're all judged by what we make happen. Learn to control the people and things around you."

My serendipitous rebuttal to that notion reads almost like an opposite or mirror image: "Try to find surprises every day. If you're never surprised it shows you're not a very good watcher/observer and your business life will be dull and consistently boring. Learn to respond as well as to act, because the very measure of our mortality is how we respond to the things that happen to us. Let your notion of control extend only to yourself."

IN OUR FAMILIES

Spiritual serendipity makes us happier in our families by helping us see our spouses and children more clearly and more individually so we can spot their needs and share their joys.

It also helps us keep the energy of humor and the excitement of flexibility and fun . . . and it reminds us that our priorities are our partners and our children, not our plans.

The plan was an early dinner to allow time for a family night activity before the younger children's bedtime. But one older boy was late getting home because he'd had to start over on his crafts project at school, which was due the following day. It would have been easy to get mad at him except for his look of excitement and pride. He'd learned to use the band saw. It was so exciting that he'd cut his piece of wood after making only one quick measurement, ruined his project, and had to start over. Redoing the project made him two hours late getting home. Our late dinner was spent in a discussion that applied the principle, "think three times, measure twice, build once" to many different aspects of life. Then, since it was late, we all went out for ice cream in our pajamas. Nothing went as planned, yet everything turned out better.

IN OUR FAITH OR COMMUNITY SERVICE

Spiritual serendipity makes us happier in our faith and service by helping us to be more people-oriented, less program-oriented.

Sensitivity and receptivity to impressions cause us to serve better and strengthen our beliefs.

I remember an incident from the period when I was consciously trying to replace my control mentality with serendipity but not doing too well at it. Some new neighbors had moved in down the street and Linda had told me that I should walk down and welcome them to the neighborhood. I had called them several times to see if I could stop by, but they were always too busy. It irritated me because I was busy and they seemed to be even more busy and I couldn't get this thing checked off of my to-do list.

I called again on another evening when I had a free hour or two and this time the woman said, "Oh, we're sorry; Jimmy's in his school play tonight."

I asked myself if there wasn't some more serendipitous solution here . . . and ended up buying a ticket for Jimmy's play, watching the first act, and spending the intermission getting acquainted with the whole family.

IN LEISURE AND PLAY

Spiritual serendipity makes us happier in the eddies of our lives as well as in the currents.

—

There is always something to do
even when there's nothing to do.
We see more possibilities, challenges, options,

feel more interests and emotions,
and live longer in the same amount of time.

———

Journal:

A gorgeous Saturday, until you look at the calendar: April 15—income tax day. Still, if I can finish my taxes during the day, we can celebrate by going out to a movie tonight. But what a day, what a fresh steady breeze, and what an idea from the six- and eight-year-olds who see kite flying as the ultimate fun.

Figures can be written and subtracted and added after dark, but kites can't be flown. What a day, what a sight to watch the children's eyes dance like their kites, and what a warm memory to carry me though the dark late hours of filling out tax returns.

———

There are many applications of spiritual serendipity—
a lot of reasons for wanting the quality,
but the reasons all telescope, umbrella, and fold down
into one word and one reason:

Spiritual serendipity is a *path*
along the unending, ever-climbing ridge
of *Joy.*

———

STEWARDSHIP

Truth never changes,
but relevance does.
divine ownership and our stewardship
have always been as true as they are now,
but perhaps never as relevant.
Because, today,
society's sentiments slide us and suck us
in opposite directions,
off toward getting and having, and particularly toward
wanting more.
History's graphs of greed, materialism, and stress
are peaking
in layers of pride, and preoccupation with possession.

We look to the light
of being and giving.
We learn who we are and whose we are,
using our gifts and our agency
to discover joy.

Now, more than ever,
The world needs stewards, and we need stewardship.

CHAPTER 6

—

ORIGINS OF STEWARDSHIP

DEFINITIONS AND ROOTS

Words sometimes evolve outside their original meaning. The English "Commonwealth," for example, is often taken to mean the common wealth—or things owned in common. The original word, however, was "common weal," which meant for the common good—things which could be used by all and not be diminished.

The word *stewardship* went through a similar evolution.

The root *tig*, which means "upward reaching"—to strive, to try—evolved into *stew*.

And the root *ware*, which means to watch out for, as in "beware," evolved into *ward*. A ward of the court in England is an heir to a title or property and is watched over until he is old enough to take over on his own. Which leads to these definitions:

Steward: One who watches over that to which he is heir, while reaching upward, acknowledging its source, remembering its giver, striving to expand it while also looking for opportunities to share and use it for the good of others.

Stewardship: The careful, responsible, and humble management of something entrusted to one's care.

My interest in the word began while I was a student. It was a time of an awakening of social responsibility, and despite the majority of students who thought and talked in terms of how much money they could make, how much power they could obtain, and how many companies and material things they could own, there was a growing minority who looked at their elite education and credentials as a responsibility, who wanted careers in nonprofit ventures and who viewed their goals in terms of contribution rather than accumulation. I was part of this minority, and to me the concept of stewardship worked better than ownership in thinking about what I wanted to do and what I wanted to have and what I wanted to be.

A good steward sees his responsibilities and his possessions and his relationships as entrustments or gifts and seeks to increase their quality and their quantity. He does not take pride but neither does he wish for less. A steward over property does not count it as superiority, but neither does he give it up or let it deteriorate. A steward over power does not use it to dominate others or elevate himself, but neither does he abdicate or shy from

the responsibility. A steward over musical or athletic talent values and develops it, and does so more to honor and share his gift than to elevate himself.

A steward over a company feels responsibility to his employees, his customers, and his stockholders and measures himself more by how he serves them than by his salary or bonuses. A steward over a promotion or position sees his title as a burden of trust rather than as a badge of pride. A steward sees himself or herself as a servant, an agent, an ambassador of the owner.

WHAT STEWARDSHIP CAN MEAN TODAY

Life is a question and stewardship is a powerful answer, or at least a new way to grasp and pull together and use the oldest, eternal answers.

Stewardship, for me personally and for my family, has become a way of looking at everything—a way that has increased peace and enhanced joy. The word or the concept is like a *lens* that turns things into a new focus—and causes me to see my life in a completely different context, to see things as they really are and, perhaps at times, even to glimpse them as God would desire them to be.

The Bible encourages us to "know the truth" and promises that "the truth shall make you free" (John 8:32). There is great freedom in the truth of stewardship. Once we mentally release ourselves from the burden, the inaccuracy, and the presumptiveness of ownership, we lighten and enlighten ourselves.

Stewardship and ownership are not just two different ways of dealing with material possessions. They are two alternate ways of thinking about everything in life—from our things and our talents, to our opportunities and options, to our relationships and our families.

The paradigm of stewardship does not suggest that we live like Gandhi or Thoreau or sell all we have and give to the poor. It doesn't ask that we

adopt a completely Spartan life or live communally. This is not a book on lifestyle. Rather, it is a book on a *mindset* or *heartset* that can free us of the cares of ownership and help us view our lives as the joyful receivers of gifts or stewardships.

Each person's stewardship is unique. Each of us has a separate and distinct set of circumstances and is capable of finding a one-of-a-kind purpose. Therefore, there is no standard formula, no pat answer. The goal of these next several chapters is not to provide ready-made, one-size-fits-all answers, but to produce perspective and stimulate thought—the very kind of thought that can work within us, prompting insight, meditation, and inspiration and helping us access unique and personal answers.

Each of us start this life in the same manner—rather naked and cold with nothing to call our own except our varying types of families. We are born to this earth, grow and learn, and then work for and receive gifts, which are ours as stewardships but still belong to something much bigger than ourselves.

Ownership in the worldly context of "I earned it, I deserve it, it's mine" is the vehicle of pride and the enemy of stewardship. The deceiver of *ownership*, in the terminology of this book, refers to the prideful form that forgets both the source and the nature of our gifts. The term *stewardship* is the accurate acknowledgment of where it all came from and whose it all is.

Consider Russell and Thoreau on the folly and the true price of ownership:

"It is the pre-occupation with possession, more than any other thing, that keeps men and women from living freely and nobly." —Bertrand Russell

"The true cost of a thing is the amount of what I call life that is required to be exchanged for it." —Henry David Thoreau

Wordsworth said it poetically, and Emerson and cummings said it bluntly:

"The world is too much with us, late and soon,
getting and spending, we lay waste to our powers.
. . . the sea that bares her bosom to the moon;

the winds that will be howling at all hours, and
are up-gathered now like sleeping flowers; for
this, for everything, we are out of tune; it moves
us not . . ."

—William Wordsworth

"Things are in the saddle and rule mankind." —Ralph Waldo Emerson

"More, more, more, more, my hell, what are we becoming, morticians?"
—e. e. cummings

Now consider a shift in attitude with Frankl and Tolstoy:

"There are more and more who have the means to live and less and less
who have meaning to live for." —Viktor Frankl

"When a man takes leave of believing in imaginary property, then only
will he make use of his true property." —Leo Tolstoy

BRANCHES OF STEWARDSHIP

Stewardship has many facets and dimensions; it is the trunk of so many
of the qualities which we seek and which we need now, more than ever, in
today's materialistic world.

For contrast, think in more depth of two trees and the branches that grow
from each.

If the name of the first tree is Ownership, then the branches it grows can
be called

- Envy
- Pride
- Ego

- Greed
- Frustration
- Win-lose competition
- Selfishness
- Stress
- Hoarding
- Vanity
- Manipulation
- Squandering
- Covetousness
- Conceit
- Overconfidence
- Condescension
- Fear
- Bitterness in tragedy
- Judgmental nature

Think about the cause and effect. Remove the notion of owning and each of these negative traits loses its very foundation—the branches can't exist without the trunk.

The simple and guiding truth of the stewardship paradigm is that we own nothing. We simply have the responsibility for the *stewardship* over things, talents, time, callings, physical bodies, and our relationships and families.

Why do we need to understand stewardship? First, because it is reality and any other paradigm or worldview is a deception; and, second, because thinking and living like stewards can rid us of the shortsighted characteristics above and replace them with their opposites. If the tree is called Stewardship, it grows very different branches:

- Humility
- Empathy
- Generosity
- Fulfillment
- Win-win cooperation/Cooperation
- Selflessness

- Peace
- Sharing
- Modesty
- Respect
- Frugality
- Satisfaction
- Meekness
- Worshipful awe
- Equality
- Courage
- Sweet acceptance
- Tolerance

Each of these qualities or branches are *effects* that can stem from the *cause* or trunk of an attitude of the heart that recognizes the truth and reality of stewardship.

—

This is not merely
A chapter on anti-materialism
(although it includes that).
Material things (misnamed possessions) are just one category
of what we don't own,
but do have stewardship over.
There are many other categories:
abilities
friends
positions
earth's beauty
opportunities
talents
children
time

spouse
physical bodies
trials
tests
loves.

If we think we own
Any of these
Or have earned them or deserve them
We are wrong,
And we're harmed by the error.
But
Never-the-less they are given to us,
they are gifts of
Stewardship
which can produce the opposite effects
of wrong, prideful ownership
And
carry us in the direction of
Gratitude and responsibility for our gifts.

Our task is to
learn to love these gifts, build them,
guide them, grow them, so that
we will come to know both their joy
and their Giver.

In a way, the idea of Stewardship defies description—
because it evolves, expands, elevates.
It begins as an attitude, a mental approach,
an aware assessment of things as they really are—
A mindset.

But as it mixes and mingles with the spirit
it becomes a feeling,

deeper and sweeter than the mind,
touching us, moving us,
reaching in to heart, to soul—
A heartset.

It intertwines with guidance, with gratitude,
and creates the peaceful speed of going slow,
expanding time,
warming the colors and textures of the everyday,
revealing unexpected, exquisite joy,
sifting and softening the strong sunlight of self
so that it absorbs and accepts and assists others
rather than reflecting off of them.

—

Stewardship is not so much a part of life, but a definition of it—a way of life. The thesis of stewardship is simple and startling. It is that, in the perspective of eternal reality, human beings own nothing except the ability to make choices.

And we make our best choices and set our wisest priorities when we recognize and understand stewardship.

—

HOW STEWARDSHIP CONNECTS TO JOY, LEADERSHIP, BALANCE, AND SERENDIPITY

t is one thing to think of a stewardship attitude as a beneficial end in itself. But it is something else again, and something more, to see its connections to other good qualities we want in our lives—qualities of joy, leadership, life-balance, and serendipity.

STEWARDSHIP AND JOY

The Egyptian God Osiris is said to ask only two questions to those who pass on: "Did you find joy?" and "Did you give joy?" An ancient rabbinical saying indicates that God asks those who die to give an accounting of "the things He made for them that they refused to enjoy."

What keeps us from enjoying God's gifts is the mistaken impression that we have earned them or that we own them. This notion encourages hoarding, overprotection, and worry and wipes away the gratitude and appreciative use of things that bring us joy.

The world has contrived and concocted a great collection of false connections . . . connections between worldly things and joy, connections of the material with the beautiful, of outer circumstances with inner happiness. This has conned and confused many of us into connecting pretentious materialism with success and respect, and into thinking that we can win happiness through bigger homes, newer boats, more expensive cars.

Joy is the objective and stewardship is the vehicle. Joy is the goal and stewardship is the plan.

Some people seem to have the capacity for deep, welling joy—the ability to be profoundly and emotionally moved by beauty, or by love and service, or by excellence and courage. In others, these capacities are muted and muffled by materialism.

In one New Testament scripture, we read of a woman, Martha, who is "cumbered about much serving . . . [and] weighed by many things to care for."[22] When we are encumbered and heavy with the pride and weight of too much, it is hard to be moved emotionally or to find room or time for simple joy. It is easy to be moved if we are *light*. The accomplishments and excellence of others can move us if we are not jealous, and the simple beauties can move us if we see and notice them and acknowledge them as the great gifts they are.

The relationship between joy and stewardship is a direct and powerful one. Joy is the objective and stewardship is the vehicle. Joy is the goal and stewardship is the plan. Joy is the end and stewardship is the means. Joy is the what and stewardship is the how.

We attended a church for a period where the lay bishop was a very wise and practical man. Professionally, he was a plumber; there was often dirt under his fingernails, and to those who were proud or judgmental, he did not make a great first impression.

Also, in that same church, there happened to be a highly trained clinical psychiatric therapist. Certain church members were going to this psychiatrist, seeking help with personal problems. Some of them were also going to their bishop for spiritual counsel. Many noticed that the plumber-pastor seemed to be rendering more help and having more effect than the expensive therapist. One of the people who noticed this was the therapist.

With some frustration, he went to the bishop one day and asked, "How do you do it? What technique do you use?" The humble bishop gave a simple answer: "I just keep asking and listening until I find out which of God's commandments they are breaking—and then I tell them to stop it. I explain that if they see their lives as taking care of what God has given them, they will be happy."

STEWARDSHIP AND LEADERSHIP

I have a friend who loves to talk about ideas. He has no interest in talking about people (he would call that gossip) and no interest in talking about the weather or everyday events (he would call that small talk). It's not that he is uninterested in people, and he loves the weather—it's just that ideas are his major interest and he doesn't really think there is enough time to talk about anything else.

I love to take long drives with this friend of mine because the time is filled with the exploration of ideas. One day, on the way back from

a trip, he asked "Why do you think that the meek will inherit the earth?" For the next several hours we worked on the question. What does inherit the earth mean? Would the meek enjoy earth's beauties and in turn care for the earth? Certainly leadership skills would be required to oversee this huge planet. Is meekness a quality of good leadership? That is certainly not the usual context. We identify effective leadership with assertiveness and aggressiveness. Aren't these opposites of meekness? Shouldn't the earth be overseen by those who had demonstrated leadership that included wisdom, intelligence, compassion, vision, courage, discipline, and love?

Yes, we decided, leadership included all of these, but great and trusted leadership included one thing more—one capstone quality that made all the other qualities work better and that allowed others to trust the leaders. This final, great quality, we decided, was meekness—defined as a humble dependency on God that would rely on the spirit and thus avoid any prideful domination.

This kind of meekness is an attitude of stewardship. A leader who sees himself as a steward over those he leads will lead with gentleness, persuasion, and patience. She will acknowledge that she is in truth a servant to those she leads. He will try to care as a steward to watch over and to lift. Such a leader is the type that others will want to be led by, that others will entrust leadership to, and thus that will inherit the earth.

In the leadership sense, stewardship is like "shepherd-ship." The shepherd leads his sheep rather than herding or pushing them around. The shepherd, or steward, cares for each sheep (or person) as an individual rather than as a flock.

The attitude of stewardship is not the only quality of leadership, but it is the capstone quality. It is the factor that can help us to lead with the guidance of the true leader, and that causes those we lead to trust our motives and to want to give us their support.

Our families provide the opportunity for one of the most useful applications of a stewardship type of leadership. Stewardship-mindful parents have clear goals for what they want to give and teach their steward

children. Their children are trusting, knowing that the parents prioritize them and will often sacrifice their own needs in order to care for, watch over, and lift them, and to help them reach their highest potentials.

STEWARDSHIP AND BALANCE

If our hearts are turned to our children, to service, to true acceptance and honoring of stewardships, then we will remove the materialism and much of the selfishness in life, replacing them with a happiness-bringing spiritual balance.

Stewardship is the attitude that brings the guidance of the Spirit into our hearts and gives us the desire to balance our lives according to a higher pattern. It is the attitude of stewardship that allows us to be comfortable living in the world without being worldly. We can live in cities surrounded by people who buy into the ownership attitude without needing to join in. We can choose instead the peace of a stewardship attitude.

I was a small boy, newly acquainted with tests and examinations in school, impressed with their gravity and seriousness, when I first heard the Sunday School answer to the question, "Why are we here on this earth?"

The answer was: "As a test."

To me, as I suspect to so many others, that was a rather ominous answer. A test was something to be feared, something where someone checked to see if you could avoid mistakes and get everything right. In my young mind then, God wanted to test us and grade us, so he made a place with a lot of hard questions and tough obstacles.

It took me many years to realize that this was a different kind of test, better named a gift of love and joy and endless possibility. If there is a test, it is to prove ourselves to ourselves and to see how much of the joy we can find.

The test mentality leads some into thinking of the world only as an obstacle course, as evil to be avoided, danger to beware of. It is this defensive orientation that makes many try to escape the world . . . from those who reject all forms of social media to hermits to everyday people who think the world is out to get them and who try in various ways to hide from it.

People sometimes misinterpret the positive couplet, "be in the world but not of the world." They take it as support for their view that the world is a bad and dangerous place to be feared and avoided. Instead, we should think of the phrase as two separate and positive admonitions: "Be in the world"—be involved, partake and enjoy, contribute and interact; "be not of the world"—avoid the materialism and worldliness that can destroy the joy.

Thus interpreted, there is such power and balance in being in but not of the world. Like a teeter-totter with weight on each end, it can keep our lives in harmony and balance. On the one hand, we're advised to be in the world—to love and appreciate others as well as their gifts and to care for all that we've been given stewardship over. On the other hand, we're asked to rise above the misuse of gifts that exist in a place made dangerous by the mixture of our agency and the opposition of evil. The couplet suggests an offense and a defense, a concentration on both doing good and avoiding bad, a challenge to seek the light side and shun the dark side. But above all, it is an invitation to put a positive interpretation on life, to live and to love as faithful, joyful stewards.

———

Worldly, Sensuous, Temporal, Physical, Materialistic, Commercial.

Words we use to describe what we hope we're not.
Yet,
what a blessing, this
physical, material earth,
a world of senses and sensation . . .

a laboratory of learning,
of expansion and expression,
of freedom and faith.

Sad then,
if we ever hate the world, or hide from it;
if we fear passion or shut out what we came here to know.

Our "physicalness," like
a horse's power (capable of hurting us or running away with us)
can be feared and killed
or bridled and enjoyed.

"Be in the world but not of it"
should be read not as
"You have to be, so try not to be"
but as two separate, joyful admonitions.
To make it so, we must remember that the world
is not our master or our identity . . . but our gift;
that we are spiritual beings entering, experiencing, enjoying
a physical extension of ourselves.
We are not physical beings who occasionally have spiritual experiences,
we are spiritual beings having a physical experience.

We must bridle, we must use with discipline,
and most of all, we must remember
Who it all belongs to.
Remembering this, and understanding and loving
our role as stewards,
makes it impossible to be "of the world"
and equally impossible not to find the joy of being "in it."

STEWARDSHIP AND SERENDIPITY

For many years, I have been giving a lecture on stewardship and ser-endipity to corporate and business groups. One night I found myself in a rural setting, giving my seminar to a group that consisted mostly of farmers. I sensed, as I spoke, that this group either didn't get it or else they needed it less than the groups I was used to.

A farmer came up afterward and convinced me that it was the lat-ter. "I enjoyed your speech," he said, "and I hadn't ever heard the word serendipity before. But you know, farmers are sort of naturally that way—we have to be." He explained that, as a farmer, he had plans of what he would like to do in a certain day, but the weather and natural conditions forced flexibility, and observing them often caused him to shift his attention to a more pressing need or a more doable project. Using my words from the seminar he said, "You can't just act on a farm," he said. "You've got to learn to react as well."

He also had a quick and insightful comment on stewardship. "Farmers mostly know they are stewards," he said. "Anyone who real-ly thinks about it knows that the land is God's, as is the water and the wind. It's our land just to use and to care for."

I drove home that night with a better understanding of why so many wise sages have warned against being too far removed from nature and from the earth, and given advice to "stay close to the soil."

I also left with a better understanding of the connections between my two favorite words: stewardship and serendipity. The words are linked in many ways. Serendipity requires spiritual awareness and guidance that may lead us in unexpected ways even as we are pursuing some other worthwhile goal. This same guidance also lies in the heart of stewardship where we acknowl-edge that we must be guided by the owner if we are to be good stewards over these things.

Early Native Americans spoke of the Great Spirit and felt that the land belonged not to individuals but to all. The acknowledgment of our status as stewards causes us to seek the very guidance that brings about spiritual

serendipity or the awareness of what God wants us to do. And the consistent pursuit of guidance and of awareness of the serendipitous directions God may have in mind for us is the best way to become worthy and effective stewards.

As our stewardships increase and expand, so does our need for spiritual serendipity. If our assignments, or entrustments, or possessions are very basic (such as a new bicycle or simple times tables in a math class), then perhaps we can do them or care for them in a rather routine, self-reliant way. But if we want to get beyond basic things or simple arithmetic into higher and freer forms, then the greater our stewardships become, and the more we need help and guidance or spiritual serendipity. We need that open, sensitive attitude in which the Spirit can speak to our spirit and help us see purer, stronger, more creative ways to multiply and magnify what we have been entrusted with.

I picture a God who might be both pleased and amused as he or she watches one of us as we sit down to set our goals and make our plans. Perhaps he would smile as he observed. Part of the smile might be an approval of our efforts to decide what we want to do and what we want to contribute. And part of the smile might be amusement in how little we know of what is in store for us and therefore how incomplete our plans usually are.

If we seek to know and understand the stewardships we have been given, and if we seek to have a constant, serendipity-like guidance in magnifying those stewardships—then perhaps the smile will also reflect pleasure in our careful caretaking.

It's one thing to talk about what stewardship is and how looking at life through a stewardship lens can help us see more clearly and perceive things as they really are. What is much harder is to actually develop a stewardship attitude within ourselves, so that stewardship becomes part of who we are rather than just part of what we understand. That is the task of the next chapter, where we will explore three keys to developing a true and personal stewardship orientation to everyday life.

THE THREE Gs OF STEWARDSHIP

There are three keys that can unlock and develop an attitude of stewardship in our lives, building within us an attitude, a perspective, and a paradigm, that can change our lives to the very core. The three keys are gratitude, generosity, and guidance and can be thought of as the three Gs of stewardship.

KEY 1: GRATITUDE

I was telling a bedtime story and praying with my three-year-old as I tucked her in one night long ago. She finished her sweet and spontaneous prayer and then she looked up at me and said, "I have two daddies," pointing at me with one hand and straight up with the other. "And I'm thankful to both of you."

Gratitude requires, first, things to be thankful for and, second, someone to be thankful to. Whomever and however we perceive God to be, we can reflect on how his or her gifts bring an unspeakable joy. This perception brings not only a willingness to live as stewards, but a deep, joyful desire to do so.

Gratitude is an indispensable part of happiness. It is also an indispensable part of stewardship. Acknowledging a higher power in all things and being grateful for all things is an indispensable part of the happiness paradigm and is the first of the three Gs of stewardship.

My Swedish maternal grandmother could not say a prayer without crying. Her gratitude welled up so deeply that sobs and heartfelt weeping were as much a part of her prayer as were words. She thanked God for everything because she believed God's hand was in everything. She couldn't think of anything good without thinking of her God.

The longer I have lived, the more I have come to appreciate the gift my grandmother had. It is an art to be able to feel gratitude as deeply as she did. The crucial beginning point in our search for this art of gratitude is the simple acceptance of the greatness of a higher power and our relative nothingness. If you approach life from a more spiritual standpoint you may feel the vastness of the universe and see that you are truly a small, small part of it all. Such a realization develops attitudes of humility, of awe, and of deep reverence.

The simple acknowledgement that we are nothing in this vast world, and that we have nothing except our stewardships, is the beginning—the indispensable starting point in the search for joy.

As we realize our nothingness, we grow in gratitude for our stewardships, which allows us to use and enjoy and grow as we care and watch over what we've been given. Most stewardships are more like a muscle than they are like a resource that can be depleted with use; the more we use our stewardships well, the stronger they will grow, the longer they will last. Just as love, trust, and joy each expand rather than deplete with use, so stewardships magnify as they are accepted and embraced.

Some have suggested that most stewardships fall into three categories: time, talents, and things. Each of these categories needs to be used well,

developed wisely, and *enjoyed*. It has been said that "there is no greater form of thanks to a giver than to find joy in what is given." Surely this applies to our stewardships.

Stewardship itself, this beautiful and peaceful attitude, this responsible, caring heartset, is not something that is earned or obtained but something that is received as a gift. Thus, part of true stewardship is gratitude for that opportunity to care and watch over something or someone.

We can prepare and position ourselves to be more qualified and receptive to the gift, but it is still a gift.

The feeling of *peace* and *joy* that comes as we exercise gratitude from our position of nothingness is the very gift that all the world wants.

One more perspective that may help:

The word *enough* is an enormously important word.

> *I have a stockbroker, estate-planner friend, who tells me that in his whole thirty-year career, he has never had a client who said "Okay, I have enough now." Instead, they say (or think), "Well, now that I have that much, it looks fairly easy (and quite important) to have more, maybe twice as much." Our definition of enough keeps increasing, prompted by media and peer pressure.*

There are two huge problems with the more, more idea:

- We default on our chance to feel gratitude. We are too busy wanting more to really notice or appreciate what we have.
- We forfeit freedom. Having enough gives us freedom, because we don't have to worry so much about necessities, and we can focus our energy on those we love, but having more and more begins to decrease our freedom, because we become so occupied in caring for, protecting, and parlaying what we have.

If we can define enough and recognize it when we have it, we earn two extraordinary blessings: gratitude (and the beauty of never taking things for granted), and the marvelous freedom of not having too much to manage.

KEY 2: GENEROSITY

As with many things, the middle step is the hardest. This second *G* tests the limits of our desire for stewardship-induced joy. We can all improve on gratitude, because for those with awareness it is natural and sensible to be thankful. Likewise, most of us welcome the third *G* of guidance in this challenging world. But the middle *G*, generosity, is perhaps somewhat less natural because until we have achieved an attitude of stewardship, our inclinations often run quite the opposite. Self-preservation, self-interest, even self-indulgence and clinging on to what we've "earned" seems instinctive. Generosity usually does not.

Yet it is clear, even obvious, that a steward must purge selfishness and develop generosity. It is clear that a good steward uses what he or she is given to serve, to give, to build, and to benefit others.

This middle *G* of generosity is the outgrowth of the other two *G*s. The more grateful we are, the more we will want to pay it forward by giving generously to others. And the more we seek guidance, the more we will be pointed toward generosity and service.

You may have heard the story or fable of a small village in Europe that was badly bombed in World War II. One of the casualties was the statue of Christ in the town square that was knocked down by the blasts and broken into pieces. Townspeople painstakingly reassembled the pieces and were able to restore the statue except for the hands, which were too broken to be fixed. Rather than sculpt new hands, the decision was to add an inscription reading: "His only hands on earth are yours."

Is any principle more certain than the simple truth that when we serve others we are lifted? Remember the original meaning of stewardship is to watch over and lift. It is interesting that when we lift others we are lifted as well! Religions around the world teach we serve God by serving others. Is it any mystery that the gift of stewardship has the common purpose of bringing joy to all—even the steward?

How do we become more generous? How do we overcome the natural tendency toward selfishness and become spiritual stewards? Generosity may be

a gift and the best pursuit may be to ask for it. But there are some things we can do that may position us better to receive and add power to our asking. One of these things is to *simplify.*

"Our life is frittered away by detail," said Thoreau. "Simplify, simplify."

Edward Abbey said he loved the desert because there was less there, so he could appreciate each tiny thing more.

> *We came home from a weekend trip some time ago and found that our home had been broken into. Drawers were pulled out. Everything was exposed. But nothing was missing. Linda remarked, "We must be poorer than I thought. Whoever broke in couldn't find a single thing worth stealing."*
>
> *There were things in our home worth stealing, of course, and I found myself with a new sense of appreciation for them as I took inventory after the break-in. All the things we cared about were there, were safe. Apparently the intruder was looking only for money, one thing there is very little of around our home.*
>
> *The anxiety I felt that day as I checked to see what was missing made me worry about simplifying and about stewardship. Was I too caught up in valuing things, in caring too much for them and thinking of them as mine?*

Do we need to get rid of all material things except our book, our dhoti, and our spectacles like Gandhi did, or move to the desert and surround ourselves only with simplicity like Edward Abbey, or sell all we have and give to the poor? Is simplifying and giving up everything material the kind of generosity that will get us to the stewardship attitude?

No. In fact, giving up everything would be, for most of us, a kind of anti-stewardship. We would be saying, "I don't want responsibility for anything." A true steward would say instead, "I want stewardship of all that I can care for and use well to serve others."

There is an interesting difference between having and needing. If we think we need all the things we have, then it is hard to give them up, hard to use them for the benefit of others. On the other hand, if we realize how little we really need, how simple our basic requirements really are, then it allows us to

be more generous. We can see what we have as stewardships and care for and develop the things we have been given without selfishly hoarding or hiding them away.

> *We've tried to give our children experiences that would increase their gratitude and their generosity—and that would help them see how little they really need. We spent one summer high in the Blue Mountains of Oregon, living a completely primitive life and building a log cabin from scratch. We all learned that we didn't need closets full of clothes or cars or television or even plumbing or electricity. We did need good, basic shelter, and we needed each other.*
>
> *Another summer we lived in a tiny mountain town in Central Mexico among shockingly poor but remarkably happy people. Our eight-year-old daughter summed up our experience on the airplane returning home. When she was asked what she learned, she answered, "That you don't need shoes to be happy."*

The kind of simplifying required to gain greater generosity and a deeper attitude of stewardship is the kind in which we give things up mentally. As stewards, we should accept and enjoy the stewardships we are given, anxious to use them and give them up as we feel inspired or as opportunities come. We should stop the aggressive pursuit of things far beyond our needs and feel deep gratitude in stewardships that we can care for well and use to serve others. When we strive to be conscious of how limited our real needs are, the act and spirit of giving becomes easier. When we see needs, sharing will be natural and when we have the chance to serve, we will be ready to serve with joy!

KEY 3: GUIDANCE

Do we want to live our lives with an analytical mentality, with a goals-and-plans approach? Certainly these are important, but there is a higher realm, a higher mentality that acknowledges the incompleteness of our finest analysis and the short-sightedness of our best goals.

To one who strives to be a steward, the world's measurements or phrases are not adequate. "A successful life." "A full life." "A life of broad experiences." "A life of service." Successful by whose standard? Full of what? Experience in what areas? Service to whom?

To those who believe in a specific purpose or some kind of life destiny and in the individuality and uniqueness of each soul and in the crucial and pivotal nature of our individual life design—the goal must be a *guided* life. We must seek a life governed by an orientation that gets us not necessarily to where we want to be or to what the world calls success, but one that gets us to our unique purpose.

It does us little good to scale the heights if we are climbing the wrong mountain or if we have propped our ladder against the wrong wall. We need direction from a higher source than our own brain or friends and family.

Reason tells us that a good steward is one who has his own thought and takes his own initiative, but who knows that the deeper things are about something more—God's heart and God's will, and the good of all. Whether we are sure there is a God or simply feel there is a power beyond our own, we are led to a mindset that is best called a guidance mentality. This kind of living is best called a guided life.

It requires faith, strong mental effort, and earnest prayer, because answers and guidance do not come automatically or easily, nor do they come in long-term blueprints for whole sections of our lives. We walk by faith, receiving confirmation from a higher spirit one step at a time.

An easy way to understand guidance mentality is to recall your biggest or most overwhelming challenge, or perhaps an assignment or change in life for which

It does us little good to scale the heights if we are climbing the wrong mountain or if we have propped our ladder against the wrong wall.

you felt unprepared or inadequate. We can all remember times when the weight of a task or challenge drove us to humility or to our knees. Abraham Lincoln said, "There are times when I am driven to my knees by the overwhelming conviction that I have nowhere else to go!"

The humility and consciousness of inadequacy caused by crisis and challenges creates a guidance mentality. We pray and ponder and meditate. We ask what should I do? How can I navigate this challenge? Thoughts and inspiration come to our minds, and we emerge with a strength and a direction that is not our own.

To strive to live each day of our lives with the same degree of humility and searching attitude is to adopt a guidance mentality.

In situations where we are overwhelmed, the world's formula of self-confidence and positive mental attitude are almost amusingly inadequate. Our strength does not come from looking into the mirror and saying, "Every day in every way I'm getting better and better" or by telling ourselves, "I can do anything." Indeed, the strength comes from an opposite approach—from saying "of myself I cannot do this, I don't know what to do." It is our humility, our nothingness, coupled with our faith in a higher power that brings the infusion of strength and insight that allows us to find our purposes and meet the challenges we are given.

Living a guided life does not require self-doubt, weakness, or insecurity. On the contrary, we are strengthened as we seek guidance and a spirit of joy and love. Simply remember that all is God's, not ours, and in remembering that we will have the necessary humility to live guided lives.

Many years ago, I had a rare opportunity to pray with a remarkable older man who taught me an extraordinary lesson about prayer.

I was praying out loud with this humble man beside me. My eyes were closed, and I was somewhat disturbed to hear the unmistakable sound of pencil writing on paper. When I finished and looked up, I saw that this senior associate had nearly filled a page of a yellow pad with writing—during the prayer! In my own immaturity, my first thought was that he was doing some sort of evaluation on my prayer. I imagined perhaps a B for content, a C for grammar, etcetera.

He noticed my consternation and said, in a completely matter-of-fact way, "I'm getting a little older now, and I sometimes worry that I will forget the answers that come in prayer if I don't take some notes."

I remember lying awake most of that night, trying to realize that prayer was communication, that we had to listen as well as ask, that the guidance received should be remembered and implemented.

Whether you pray in a formal or informal way or use meditation to clear your mind and feel peace, listen and feel and remember thoughts and guidance that come to your mind and heart. And just maybe grab your pen and paper to take a few notes (regardless of your age).

"Ask and listen" is a wonderful motto for communication with those around you as well as with a higher power. When we ask and listen we learn, we show esteem, we grow, and we share.

That same man who took notes on prayer taught me how he established a pattern while yet a young man in which he asked for guidance each morning and then gave an accounting each evening as he knelt in prayer before retiring—an accounting of how he had tried to follow the guidance during the day.

The point is that guidance must never be taken lightly. When we ask for it, when we receive it, we must be willing to remember it, to follow it, to do it!

———

THE OXYMORONS OF STEWARDSHIP

Oxymoron:
A word pair or phrase that works even though
(literally) one word
contradicts the other:
pretty ugly
freezer burn
jumbo shrimp
Sometimes they creep into our sports terminology:

backup forward
two-center offense.
The interesting thing about oxymorons
is that while the individual words conflict,
the two-word phrase is useful and workable.
Stewardship of the Heart as an attitude,
creates three workable, useful oxymorons:

confident humility
We are confident because we know who we are
and how to impact the world for good,
yet humble because we understand our nothingness.

frugal generosity
Stewardship means caring for what we have,
and growing it,
but it also means giving it
and not valuing it into ourselves.

independent reliance
We learn to think and to self-determine,
even as we depend and rely on
the guidance of those we trust
and of the spirit.

—

CHAPTER 9

SPIRITUAL STEWARDSHIP

Paradigm shifts of a life-changing nature happen when people perceive and accept the spiritual side of life. Eternal truths about who we are and where we came from can change how we see ourselves and how we view our lives. In turn, the way we view life changes how we live life—altering what we think is important and motivating us to reach higher and strive to be better.

Change a person's eye prescription and you may change his sight, thus improving the clarity with which he sees his surroundings. But when you change a person's paradigm you may change his *insight*, thus improving the clarity with which he sees himself and his life.

Insight is a fascinating word because it implies an *inner* sight—and we realize with our "real eyes" things not otherwise known—things deeper and more permanent than the surface—things that can change how we live as well as how we see.

THE DIVINE PLAN

Early in this book, a scripture was mentioned that says "Adam fell that man might be (mortal), and men are (mortal) that they might have joy."

Whatever you might believe or not believe about scripture, about God, and about Adam and Eve, it all certainly provides a story-basis with which to explore things like purpose and plan, and good and evil.

If there is a God, most of us would want that God to be benevolent and interested in us and in our happiness, and we would hope that in the scope of complete divine knowledge, things that make little sense to us make perfect sense to God and form some kind of ultimate plan for this world and for all of us who live upon it.

If God's logic is higher but similar to ours, it would stand to reason that there is some purpose or plan for our mortal lives, that mortality is some kind of preparation for a greater world to come, and that this earth is some kind of complex school wherein we learn, or can learn, the things that will ultimately make us happy.

The stewardship paradigm simplifies decisions, because we simply choose the greater stewardship—and this impacts our choices, big and small.

It seems clear that one key part of life is learning to make wise choices. When we are children, we learn simple things like "don't run into the street." As teenagers we learn life skills and how to navigate friendships and feelings. As adults we enter careers and start families. All along the way there are challenges, oppositions, good choices, and bad choices. We learn that part of our growth comes from making choices—both good and bad ones—and experiencing opposition, challenges, and heartache. Perhaps this earth is a perfectly designed school or laboratory where we can learn for ourselves how to love, how to find peace, and how to find joy.

These destinations or discoveries are not easy and the paths to them are not obvious, but if we believe that all the elements are here, all the opposing forces, all the choices, all the possibilities, then we can approach our lives as a high-consequence puzzle, we can look for the pieces and try to assemble them into the joy and purpose of this place.

I have found that the stewardship paradigm simplifies decisions, because we simply choose the greater stewardship—and this impacts our choices, big and small.

A short illustration of the small and the large: It was NFL playoff time and I had plans to watch a game with friends—until twelve-year-old Saydi reminded me there was a daddy-daughter activity at her school. I was really into that game, but the biggest stewardship was Saydi. Small choice made. A few years earlier, right after a couple of big victories in the political consulting firm that I had founded, we were asked as a family to go to England for three years to supervise six hundred young, full-time volunteers who were doing humanitarian and service work, largely in the poorest areas of London. It would mean a lot of missed professional opportunities and entail some major personal sacrifices, but it was clearly a more important stewardship than what we were doing. Big decision made.

THE REALNESS OF EVIL

Scripture and legend hints of a "fallen angel" who became the opponent of God. And whether or not you believe literally in either one, the juxtaposition of the story can help us to understand happiness and its opposites.

In the scriptural story, the fallen angel is banished from heaven and thus begins the ongoing and lasting story of his demonic and unceasing struggle to win us to him and take us from God.

How does evil go about the objective to take us from God and to control the world God has made? Does it involve temptation? Is it connected to selfishness and insensitivity? Does it emphasize the physical and deny the spiritual?

Does evil have a strategy or a game plan?

We know something of evil's nature. It is unwise to dwell on it or become overly aware of it. C. S. Lewis said, "There are two great mistakes we can make with regard to the devil—one is to think too much about him, the other is not to think enough about him." It is always helpful (and healthy) to know an opponent's strategy well enough to effectively fight or avoid it.

Evil's plan is to use our agency or choices against us. The goal has always been to enslave us. The Fallen Angel story says he tried to do so by taking away our freedom of choice. Failing to do that, evil now tries to use our agency against us by influencing us to focus on *getting and keeping and hoarding—and having*—all of which enslave us.

Evil's plans are always counter to God's. It tried to counter the divine plan of agency with force and now tries to counter selfless stewardship with a counter perspective of selfish ownership. Where a stewardship mentality can build cooperation and humility and thus liberate us, an ownership mentality builds pride and a lonely form of incarceration.

How well is evil's strategy working? Look around! People spending more than they earn—and spending it before they earn it; judging themselves and others on how much they have; becoming jealous and envious of each other based on the comparion of possessions. Bumper stickers say, "He who dies with the most toys wins" and "I owe, I owe, so off to work I go." A pretentiousness reigns in which we spend more than we can afford for houses bigger than we need, or for cars and clothes designed to impress.

The counter-plan of ownership involves counterfeit connections between things and joy. But they are false connections that don't work. What ownership provides is pride, worry, selfish "protectiveness," and dangerous feelings of independence from any higher law or power.

The antidote to evil's poison of pride is the acknowledgment of divine ownership of all, and the joyful acceptance of our favored role as children, stewards, and heirs!

SPIRITUAL LEVELS

There are four levels on which people can live, depending on their paradigms. The highest level, level 4, is stewardship:

Level 1: The world owes me a living.

Level 2: I own, you own. I deserve what I've got and you deserve what you've got.

Level 3: Where much is given, much is expected. I've been given much, so I must give back.

Level 4: All is God's. Through my stewardships I can assist in divine purposes.

As noble as the third level is, it does not plug in to spiritual power as level 4 does. On level 3 we might seek guidance by asking, "What of mine can I give to others?" On level 4 we would ask, "What would the divine have me do with this since it is His already?"

AN ANTIDOTE FOR PRIDE

We sometimes need two different words for pride because it means two different things—one positive and one negative. When we are proud of our children or take pride in our work, it works for us. But when pride is an overstatement of our own control, ownership, and independence, it works against us and against our happiness. That second, negative form of pride is the operating factor as well as the result of an ownership mentality.

Pride is ugly, saying, "if you succeed more than I do, I am a failure; if I succeed more than you, you are a failure." Pride keeps us from learning new things, since doing so sometimes requires us to admit that we were wrong.

Pride is (sometimes) the story of the rich and successful looking down on those with less. But pride can also live with those who have less, resenting and criticizing and judging those who have more. Pride centers on competitiveness and enmity, which pulls us apart and divides us from others.

Pride stems from the false concept of ownership. Thinking we own things breeds enmity because if someone else owns it, we can't, and if we win, someone else loses. With stewardship, we appreciate others' gifts as much as our own; we are increasingly humble as more is entrusted to us, more inclined to use what we have in service; the only pride we feel is pride in and praise of the divine.

If the illness is prideful ownership, then the antidote is an attitude of stewardship and humility.

CHAPTER 10

—

STEWARDSHIP
OVER SELF

Anyone adopting a stewardship attitude would quickly agree that the first and foremost thing we have stewardship over is ourselves. Taking care of yourself is a beginning, not in the self-centered, only-my-needs-matter-to-me way, but in the view of knowing that your own body, mind, and soul is your first stewardship and first gift from God.

Benjamin Franklin took stewardship of himself by creating a list of the things he wanted to become and working at them systematically. Our exercise programs and diets are ways of taking care of our bodies, as mind-games and reading and other stimulation are ways to care for our brains.

Taking care of our spirits and of our character is often a bit harder. We need to be very clear on who we are and on who we want to become. One way to do this is to develop a personal mission statement or vision statement that symbolizes who you want to be and what you want to become.

Stephen Covey, author of the bestselling self-help book of all time, The 7 Habits of Highly Effective People, *also happened to be Linda's and my personal friend and mentor for more than forty-five years. One night at dinner he asked us if we had a personal mission statement and a family mission statement. I showed him the vision statement our company had developed for business, and he said, in essence, "Fine—most companies have these now, but by far the most important vision statement you can have is for yourself and for your family."*

The outgrowth was that Linda and I and our children developed a family vision statement that still influences us all every day. It started as a one-page essay that we wrote together when most of our kids were teenagers. We went on a little weekend retreat and mixed play with serious brainstorming. We started by listing words that we thought should describe our family and the identity and definition we wanted our family to have. Later, in a family meeting, we reduced and condensed the essay into one paragraph and, finally, worked on it together and got it down to one three-word mantra:

"Broaden and Contribute."

To us it essentially meant get the best education and experience you can and then give back to society and to all the institutions that have made you what you are.

Developing individual mission statements was harder, but we encouraged each of our children to do so, and Linda and I tried to lead the way.

As I sat down to work on my own, I realized that I knew, in general terms, what I wanted and what I wanted to be. But coming up with the specifics and putting it in a form that was powerful enough to become part of me was a challenge. I've tried different approaches over the years and it is a work in progress (which is perhaps what it always should be).

One attempt had to do with turning my name and my initials into a memorable overview of my vision for myself. I liked my initials, RE, because they could be put into a format that summarized many of the most important things I wanted to be and to do:

REmember,

REjoyce,

REmain,

REceive,

REpent,

RElease,

REtain,

REalize.

You may want to find some connecting and symbolic framework like this for your personal mission statement, but the important thing is that you spend some concentrated time pondering what is important to you and try writing it in a way you will remember. As we think and ponder the kind of persons we want to be, we will come to understand that being a steward over ourselves will lead and guide and push us to recognize our stewardship over everything that we have responsibility for in this life.

SYNERGICITY

"I only acknowledge what science can prove,"
said an acquaintance of mine,
proud of his commitment to logic and reason.
"I believe what I can understand."
Do you understand love? I asked, or intuition, or beauty?
Can a worm explain a thunderstorm?

Can't we leave room in our tiny brains for the possibility of magic,
and for the faith that there is more
than the narrow dimension of what humans grasp?
Are not the things that defy logic more interesting
than the things that follow it?
Are not the questions more intriguing than the answers?

How can 2 plus 2 equal 5, or 8? (we name that magic "Synergy")
How can a butterfly flapping its wings in Argentina
affect the weather in New York City?
(we name that magic Synergicity)
The most exciting things are the ones we can name but can't understand,
And sometimes, they can even
Be combined.

CHAPTER 11

ORIGINS OF
SYNERGICITY

Consider two statements:

1. One plus one can equal three (with cooperation and love, the total can be greater than the sum of its parts).
2. Despite our obsession with independence, two of the most obvious facts of the universe are our dependence and interdependence, and the interconnectedness of everything.

If you find these two notions thought-provoking, and if there is an intuitive ring of truth in both of them, you are ready to dive deeper into the third alternative of synergicity. This section will explore it as an attitude, as a paradigm, and as an exciting new way to view everyday life.

Synergicity, as explained earlier in The Big Reveal, is a combination and a hybrid of *synergy* and *synchronicity.*

I had come to love the word synergy *in my early years as a management consultant, and was fond of telling managers how much more they could accomplish if they worked in tandem and with teamwork so that the collective result was greater than the sum of everyone working individually. I called it the "magic of synergy," but candidly, to me in those days, synergy was something you planned and built deliberately by getting people together and tapping into each other's strengths.*

As the years passed, however, I began to realize that there was another kind of deeper, logic-defying magic where things connected and catalyzed each other without any planning or particular effort by anyone. It was as though some higher intelligence was orchestrating things that were vast and had connections beyond our understanding, and certainly beyond my analysis or management theory. The best ideas came in flashes rather than as the logical conclusion of some analytical process; something that happened in one branch of a company produced unexpected results in another branch; a delay on one thing made possible a more important acceleration of another thing. The best word I could find for this kind of beneficial but acausal relationships between things was synchronicity.

And the best examples of these words didn't even come from business or from the companies or campaigns I consulted; they came from my marriage. Linda and I, both strong-willed and opinionated, spent the first few years of our marriage wishing we could be more alike. (Specifically, I wished she could be more like me and she wished I could be more like her.) But gradually we began to see not only the synergy in our differences, but the synchronicity. Her perspective broadened mine and my opinion modified or honed hers. We started

*relishing rather than resisting our differences and we started to learn
to combine rather than compete.*

Synergicity, then, is the paradigm alternative to *independence*. Instead of
implying that we don't need others, it suggests that we are all interdependent
and interconnected and that people working together can accomplish much
more than the total of what everyone could do by themselves. Instead of
claiming that we can stand alone, it suggests that we are always better off if
we stand together with those we love and if we acknowledge both our mutual interdependency and our dependency on something higher.

Instead of exclusive focus on individualism, *synergicity* focuses on family,
friends, communities, and connections. Instead of looking for ways to do
better than others, it aims at ways of doing better *with others*. Instead of
striving to do things in spite of the circumstances around us, it prompts us to
do things in harmony with the realities around us. And instead of the goal of
lifting ourselves by our bootstraps to the objectives we have set, it teaches us
to let ourselves be lifted by nature, by others, and by the spiritual influences
that surround us.

A LIBERATING ALTERNATIVE
TO INDEPENDENCE

Unfortunately, independence has become such a commonly accepted goal
that we seem to almost worship the concept. It is certainly the topic and
the main thrust of hundreds of self-help books and countless life coaches.
Somehow our society has elevated being independent to iconic levels, and it
has become one of the key yardsticks by which we measure success.

In short, independence has become the assumed objective of almost everyone, and the obsession of many. The obsession leads to disproportionate
time and thought on self and begins to suck our attention toward social
media accounts, body image, me-time, and selfies.

While some aspects of independence may be worth pursuing (like a level of financial independence, independent thinking, and having one's own

opinion), we must recognize that a broad quest for independence, particularly emotional and spiritual independence, is a deception of the first order. The simple fact is that we are completely dependent on circumstances and situations and vastly interdependent on each other.

Yet today's culture seems to encourage the impossible goal of standing alone and doing everything for ourselves. We should turn that goal completely around and, instead, look for opportunities to serve others, to let them serve us, and to become good givers and good receivers. We can recognize that we are living on a higher level than independence when we depend on family and friends even as we invite them to depend on us.

In doing so, we open ourselves up to others as well as to a higher source. We admit our vulnerability, weaknesses, and needs. We feel the calming honesty of acknowledging our own nothingness and the *everythingness* of humanity as a whole and of the divine.

SYNERGICITY IS ALL ABOUT TRUST, TIMING, AND OTHER PEOPLE

The deceptive lens of independence is always focused on self, trying to make things happen when and how you want them to, depending only on yourself, and not needing to wait for or rely on or even trust other people. Synergicity is exactly opposite. It's all about others; it's about helping and being helped. It's about trusting and depending on those around us and on a higher guidance—and looking for spiritual connections and timing in all things.

The two are direct opposites. A person striving for independence is preoccupied with his own ability, while one seeking synergicity is aware first of his own vulnerability. Independence flows toward pride and overconfidence, while synergicity is awed and humbled and in wonder at the greatness of things beyond ourselves. Independence demands self-reliance, while synergicity acknowledges how we completely rely on Mother Earth

for everything, for our very breath. An independence-seeker gravitates to win-lose mindsets and tends to explain things in terms of opportunity, ability, good fortune, or the simple luck of being in the right place at the right time; synergicity-seekers look for win-win and sense that there are more connections and more divine design than we can imagine. Independence relies on a personal recipe of "work" and "plan," while synergicity depends additionally on a formula of "watch" and "pray."

Mother Teresa taught of the folly of independence and the joy of synergicity:

"If we have no peace, it is because we have forgotten that we belong to each other . . . Spread love everywhere you go. Let no one ever come to you without leaving happier."

And a woman named Barbara Dillingham understood the interconnectedness:

"Life is not a path of coincidence, happenstance, and luck, but rather an unexplainable, meticulously charted and choreographed course for one to touch the lives of others and make a difference in the world."

Synergicity is about finding links with others and discovering opportunities in the unexpected timing with which things occur in our lives. It is about acknowledging that there is a realm that not only knows what to give us for our best good, but when to give it. We learn to trust a higher power, and to look for a time frame beyond our perspective. We learn to ask searching and sincere questions, such as:

- Why did this happen now?
- What can I gain from this, and what can I give from this?
- Why did I come into contact with this person?
- Why am I having this experience, and what good can I take from it or make of it?

Synergicity is how we examine our lives. It is how we seek and find our true purposes. It is how we strive to bring our lives into harmony with that purpose. It is how we discover opportunities both to give and to receive.

Over the years, Linda and I have served on the boards and worked with nonprofit organizations that send individuals and families on humanitarian expeditions to Third World villages to help build schools or clinics or irrigation systems and to create personal connections between people from different nations and backgrounds. We became quite addicted to these expeditions because of what they did for our kids' attitudes and perspectives. One of the things that always amazed me was how quickly our children connected with the children in the villages. Even if they come from different worlds and speak different languages, children seem to almost instantly discover much more that they have in common, and they are laughing and playing together long before the adults make any of the same connections. On one such expedition, I remember thinking that all we really have to do to understand and achieve more synergicity is to watch and learn from children and make friendships as naturally as they do.

For a separate illustration of this, take a minute and visit a coffee shop on YouTube at https://www.youtube.com/watch?v=Pm12mTIUJss. See the beautiful perspectives of children on friendships and what really matters.

CHAPTER 12

———

THE SYNERGY PART
OF SYNERGICITY

The idea and notion of independence has two critical flaws. The first is that it relies on "self" instead of acknowledging our need for help, asking for it, and seeking it. The second is that independence often tries to operate without awareness of the bigger picture, failing to look for a higher and longer-range timing in everything.

The alternative of synergicity, particularly the first half of the word, is all about seeking help, direction from the divine and from others—seeking help instead of trying not to need it!

DEFINITIONS

To understand the mindset of synergy, let's revisit our explanations and look at some hybrid definitions gathered from various dictionaries:

Synergy: The interaction of two or more agents or forces so that their combined effect is greater than the sum of their individual parts.

Synergy: (pronounced SIN-ur-jee) From the Greek *sunergia* meaning cooperation, or *sunergos*, meaning working together efficiently.

Synergy: (from the Greek *synergos*, meaning working together, circa 1660) Refers to the phenomenon in which two or more discrete influences or agents acting together create an effect greater than that predicted by knowing only the separate effects of the individual agents. The opposite of synergy is antagonism, the phenomenon where two agents in combination have an overall effect which is less than that predicted from their individual effects.

Synergy can also mean:

- A mutually advantageous conjunction where the whole is greater than the sum of the parts.
- A dynamic state in which combined action is favored over the sum of individual component actions.
- Behavior of whole systems unpredicted by the behavior of their parts taken separately.

These secular and scientific definitions are interesting—but not nearly as interesting as when the word takes on a spiritual dimension. In its original, earliest form, the word was used to describe a spiritual concept. *Synergism* stems from the 1657 theological doctrine that humans will cooperate with the Divine Grace in regeneration. The term began to be used in the broader, non-theological, sense by 1925.

Spiritual synergy becomes a remarkable, even awesome, term that can mean the power and efficiency of working with others and with the divine. In this book, it is both a mindset and a heartset.

As we broaden our thinking and consider the concept of synergy on several levels, we begin to see the many relationships where it can apply:

1. The synergy between you and other people.
2. The synergy between husband and wife (the essential definition of a good marriage).

3. The synergy between your brain, body, and spirit (whole soul synergy).
4. The synergy between you and a higher power.

Exploring the various applications and nuances of synergy makes it an ever-more compelling word and is the logical first step in grasping the third alternative of synergicity and understanding the severe limits and loneliness of the independence paradox.

BE MORE THAN WHAT YOU CAN BE, AND DO MORE THAN WHAT YOU CAN DO

It is common to hear someone say something like, "We all have limits and limitations, right? And all we can do is all we can do!" or "It is what it is."

The fact is that we limit ourselves by accepting the idea and the ideal of independence. When we depend only on ourselves, our limits are finite and apparent. And we often fall short of what is needed in a situation—of getting what we need and giving what others need. We suffer in silence, feeling inadequate and sometimes a little helpless and hopeless.

That is the very point: help and hope do not come from independence. Hope comes from dependence on a higher power, and help comes from *inter*dependence with other people. Once we get over the limiting attitude of independence, we can begin to develop real synergy—with other people and the more spiritual side of existence.

Working together, sharing ideas and combining complementing talents, people can do amazing things—more than expected, more than the sum of what they could do individually or independently. In business, the prime reason that companies merge is that they have complementing strengths or assets that allow their bottom line to expand beyond the combination of their separate profits. In nature there are countless examples of synergy, which often include a mutual dependency called symbiosis. Clownfish,

for example, have a synergistic or mutualistic relationship with sea anemones. The anemones repel clownfish predators by stinging them with their tentacles. A protective layer on the clownfish's skin protects them from the sting. At the same time, clownfish scare off butterflyfish that try to eat the anemones.

In person-to-person relationships there is something about synergy that defies mathematics, something magical, something emotional and exciting that goes beyond the practical and beyond what can be added up or figured out. It is, essentially, a way of surpassing your personal capacity and reaching levels and doing things that are otherwise impossible.

TWO WAYS TO FIND MORE SYNERGY IN YOUR LIFE

First: ASK more! When you ask other people for help, for advice, for input, you are creating opportunities for synergy. You are bringing the minds and hands of others into the equation, and the combined result of their actions and thoughts and yours will be greater than the sum of yours and theirs taken separately.

Asking your spouse more often what he or she thinks or needs or feels can be the beginning of more synergy in your marriage. Asking your children more often what they think or need can be the beginning of more synergy in your family.

Asking your body what it needs, and listening to it—and asking your spirit what it needs—begins a process leading to soulful synergy and completeness.

Asking for guidance is the most powerful asking of all. As mentioned earlier, of all the admonitions of scripture, to ask is the most repeated! Think about that: Of all the things God tells us to do, the most often repeated is the simple admonition: ASK! When we ask the divine for inspiration and guidance, as well as for the things we need or want, we open the door to untold blessings. Many of us understand this better when we become parents because we all long for our children to ask us for our advice, for our counsel

and help. We want them to take advantage of our desire to share what we know with them and to serve them.

Second: THINK of yourself in a different way—never alone and always interconnected. As you go about your daily life, think how glad you are that you are NOT independent—that you are dependent on so much and on so many, and that you are interdependent with everyone and everything. Begin to see yourself as fitting into something so big and so wonderful and so awesome that you can scarcely imagine it. Adopt the lovely, humble feeling of dependence and interdependence.

This will cause you to appreciate others more, to notice them more, to seek their feedback and feelings and to enjoy and welcome their input and impressions. And perhaps even more importantly, it will cause you to notice and appreciate more the nature of divine blessings and guidance in your life.

These simple changes in how you ask and how you think constitute a powerful shift in your mindset and your heartset; and it is guaranteed to make you happier.

CHAPTER 13

THE SYNCHRONICITY
PART OF
SYNERGICITY

A gain, let's start with some of our own definitions derived from dictionaries and combined to more fully illustrate the concept:

Synchronicity: The experience of two or more events that occur in a meaningful manner, but which are causally unrelated. In order to be synchronous, the events must be related to one another conceptually, and the chance that they would occur together by random chance must be very small.

Synchronicities are patterns that repeat in time. The word *synchronicity* references the gears or wheels of time, though the actual concept of synchronicity cannot be scientifically proven. One can only record synchronicities as they occur and watch the patterns of behavior that create them.

Synchronicity is an explanatory principle according to the word's creator, Carl Jung. Synchronicity explains "meaningful coincidences."

"Synchronicity is the coming together of inner and outer events in a way that cannot be explained by cause and effect and that is meaningful to the observer."—Carl Jung

Some of these definitions may sound a little esoteric or theoretical. But in fact, the word should be very practical and approachable because all of us experience simple examples of it in our everyday lives. Little things that seem to happen for a reason, but you can't reason out what the reason is—small coincidences or connections. You think of someone for the first time in years and run into them a few hours later. An unusual phrase you'd never heard before jumps out at you three times in the same day. On a back street in a foreign country you bump into a college roommate. A book falls off the shelf at the bookstore and it's exactly what you need.

Are these, as skeptics suggest, selective perception and the law of averages playing itself out? Or are they, as Carl Jung, the Swiss psychiatrist and psychoanalyst, believed, a glimpse into the underlying order of the universe? It was he who coined the term *synchronicity* to describe what he called the "acausal connecting principle" that links mind and matter. He said this underlying connectedness "manifests itself through meaningful coincidences that cannot be explained by cause and effect."

THE MINDSET AND HEARTSET OF SYNCHRONICITY

The word *synchronicity* has attracted somewhat of a cult following over the years. It is the name of a magazine and of an album by the rock group *The Police*; it has developed a kind of mystical and new-age sort of context.

However, when we add the spiritual dimension, the word can come to mean much more. It can mean recognizing a divine hand in everything

and trusting a deeper timing. It can suggest to the mind the interconnect-edness of everything in the universe. To we humans, who see such a narrow slice of things, and who each live in our own little worlds, things seem un-connected and random. Coincidences seem to be things of chance. But, in truth, everything is connected, and all of us are linked to each other and to a grand design and marvelous plan.

I heard a phrase once that stuck in my mind: "The speed of going slow." Maybe it stuck with me because of its apparent self-contradiction, but it seemed more than that. I somehow knew it was a true principle or at least a true possibility. I knew there were some days when I felt a calmness and peace that seemed to make all the traffic lights turn green just as I got to them and somehow eliminated lines and precipi-tated shortcuts to whatever I needed. There was no hurry or rush, but I got where I was going easily and efficiently and finished things with-out stress. And when some way was blocked or something was pulled from my reach, I had no trouble letting it go and didn't mind changing gears and moving in a different direction with a quiet assurance that there would be better timing on another day. Gradually, I learned to call this feeling synchronicity *and to look for it and develop it.*

"If you pay attention at every moment, you form a new relationship to time. In some magical way, by slowing down, you become more efficient, productive, and energetic, focusing without distraction on the task in front of you. Not only do you become immersed in the moment, you become that moment." —Michael Ray

This perspective from Kristine Maudal and Even Fossen says it well: "Leaders of the past who made great achievements knew the importance of going slow. The founder of the Roman Empire, Augustus, would use the Latin phrase *Festina Lente*. This translates to: 'Make haste, slowly.' It served as a reminder for Augustus to perform activities with a proper balance of urgency and diligence."[23]

SYNCHRONICITY IS ALL ABOUT THE TIMING, EVEN THE PERFECT TIMING

"Timing is everything." "Being in the right place at the right time." There are so many catchphrases about timing, because we know, instinctively, that timing is the key to almost everything. In sports, the difference between a great player and an ordinary one is timing. And in life, the difference between success and failure so often comes down to timing.

The problem is that, in the big game of life, we try to control timing, but actually have so little ability to manage it. A whole, giant industry has grown up called "Time Management." But we don't actually manage time—we only hope to manage ourselves within time, trying to make good use of our time, and to spend it on important things.

Time is measured relative to the earth's rotations and revolution—all put into play by some higher power and held there by nature's laws. When we are in sync with divine timing and nature, and willing to trust in them rather than always wishing we could set the timetable, we begin to see and understand spiritual synchronicity.

We can no more determine when will meet someone who will become a lifelong friend than we could tell the earth when or how to spin. A person may want a certain thing or occurrence right now—such as a promotion, a raise, a marriage, a child, or a talent—only to have it come later and in a different form or variation than he had imagined. And we so often find, with hindsight, that the timing was exactly right, that it happened in the moment and sequence that was best, even though we could not have predicted it. When we trust in a divine timing, we begin to worry less in the abstract and live more in the moment.

Like children, we often want instant gratification, or for something to happen just as we imagined it and right when we want it. This is another example of a "me, me, me" attitude. The timetable of life is different and if we can learn to trust divine timing, and to watch for and perceive and purpose and opportunity to learn as events unfold before us, life becomes much more exciting and complete.

With this attitude, little synchronicities happen to us more often. Something is there when we need it—a person or an idea or an answer. We start to connect the things that happen to us and around us to our needs and to others' needs. We start trusting our impressions and our nudges and begin to see them as promptings from something divine. We begin to notice bigger patterns and connections.

Once we begin to notice simple examples of synchronicity in our daily lives, we can begin to harness the quality and increase its frequency.

Often, when I think of people I need to call—but jot it down on a list and try to call them later—they don't answer. But if I call just when I think of it, just when the prompt comes, I always seem to get right through. For me, that is the greatest value of a cell phone. When someone comes into my mind, I call and there they are. If I look at the impression to call as a spiritual nudge or a tiny inspiration and if act on it, the timing works, the synchronicity occurs.

Having a too-rigid agenda of our own, and trying to force things to happen within our own timetable and according to our own convenience rarely works. All this does is make us feel like we are exerting great effort, but going against the current or the flow. If we can just slow down a little, open our minds and our hearts, and look for synchronicity, seeking to feel nudges and impressions, we seem to find a channel or a current that brings about what should happen. This doesn't mean we don't have a plan; we just keep flexible the timing of what we feel we want to do and stay open to what comes into our path and our minds. We realize there is a greater force working for our good and the good of those we meet each day.

In this light, synchronicity ties closely to serendipity in that it is our awareness and our perspective that brings them both to us. Going slow and watching for opportunities to serve often lead to a better purpose than we would find otherwise. Synchronicity also ties to stewardship in that it involves seeing ourselves as stewards within some larger plan for humanity. But always, and paramount, spiritual synchronicity involves looking for the interconnectedness of events, people, and timing in all.

HOW TO FIND MORE
SYNCHRONICITY IN YOUR LIFE

The best way to get more synchronicity, of course, like the way to get any blessing, is to ASK for it in prayer or seek it in meditation. If we ask to see connections, to feel the links, and to recognize divine timing in our lives, we will become ever more perceptive and in tune. We will welcome "coincidences" and we will understand that they are much more than that. We will develop the mindset and heartset that attracts synchronicity.

Seeking for this kind of spiritual synchronicity can open our spiritual eyes. God's own advice and admonition is "watch and pray," (see Mark 13:33) and indeed, once again, those are the two keys—ask for it and watch for it.

The concept of synergy and the quality of synchronicity are marvelously interesting notions, but each has limitations, and neither is a complete alternative to the deceiver of independence. But they can combine—merging into a third rescuer: synergicity.

———

CHAPTER 14

COMBINING SYNERGY AND SYNCHRONICITY INTO SYNERGICITY

The reason I like to combine the word *synchronicity* with the word *synergy* is that the combined word *synergicity* suggests that everything is connected and within a higher control than we can comprehend and that when we work together and in sync with that higher power and with each other, things get better and both the timing and the results become more in line with ultimate possibility.

Synchronicity is all about seeing opportunities and connections and unexpected timing from broader perspectives rather than trying to force everything to fit our idea of when and how things should happen. The paradigm of synergicity can be liberating—even magical.

A WORKING DEFINITION
OF SYNERGICITY

Synergicity, a spiritual connection of synergy and synchronicity, can be defined as:

A state of mind and spirit that acknowledges (indeed, celebrates) one's complete dependency on higher powers and complete interdependency and cooperation with other people, resulting in enhanced results; an attitude and approach that seeks divine purpose and looks for guidance in all things, particularly in the timing and interconnectedness of life events.

Another way to define a word is by what it isn't and by the notion that it rejects. Synergicity is the antithesis of independence. It does not seek win-lose competitiveness or embrace the prideful attitude of not needing others or the false ideal of "going it alone."

It is pursued by changing our attitude and awareness. It is not earned or deserved or accomplished. It is a clarity available through inspiration. Thus, it must be asked for as well as worked for and *thought for*.

THE POWER AND PURSUIT OF
SYNERGICITY AND NOTHINGNESS

I suggest that, for starters, you make in your own mind a personal declaration of interdependence with other people and a declaration of divine dependence on a higher source. Just acknowledging your own lack of independence is a good first step. It brings a type of peaceful humility wherein there is much less stress. It allows us to start turning things over to a higher power and it increases our faith and our hope. It allows us to follow the admonition to "Cast thy burden upon the Lord" (see Psalm 55:22).

Sometimes just understanding one's own nothingness is the beginning of a glorious humility that liberates us from pride, selfishness, and loneliness. Nothingness, as it turns out, is not a negative thing; in fact, it is a powerful thing that opens to us great worlds of promise.

My introduction to the word nothingness *came in a prayer. I was attending a conference that started and ended each of its sessions with a prayer. The older gentlemen who offered the closing prayer apparently felt the need to remind the leaders that it was about something bigger than them—that it was the purpose and cause and goals of the organization that mattered. In his prayer, he said, "Please bless the officers on this stand with a realization of their own nothingness." Something about the way he said it made it clear that his request was not a put-down but a simple acknowledgment that the cause and purposes of the organization were more important than the individuals running it and that they were a part of something bigger than themselves.*

Humility gives us gratitude and causes us to rejoice. Realizing the power of the divine and how dependent we are can fill us with love and peace. Feeling our nothingness allows us to be more observant of things as they are and less preoccupied with things as we want to make them. And sensing that nothingness brings peace that leads us to love and teach love in our families and communities.

Nothingness is the trigger of synergicity! When we are in this state of mind, we look for and submit to divine timing and notice tender mercies and nudges. We reach out to work synergistically with others, look for win-win solutions, and find better ways rather than insisting on our way.

SYNERGICITY AS AN ACCURATE LENS ON LIFE

Synergicity is a lens through which we try to view the world—with everything interconnected, everything potentially benefiting from everything else, and in one way or another depending on everything else.

In its fullest form, this third rescuer of joy is a combination of the words *synergy* and *synchronicity,* with a little bit of *symbiosis* thrown in for good measure. It can be defined as a paradigm in which we acknowledge divine dependence, mutual interdependence, and respect the interconnectedness of all things, times, and occurrences within the framework of the real known and unknown universe.

CHAPTER 15

THE EQUATION FOR SPIRITUAL SYNERGICITY

Already mentioned was the notion that synergy can seem to defy mathematics by producing situations where one plus one equals three.

But in another way, a mathematical equation can tell us accurately just how to obtain synergicity. Indeed, there is a constant and reliable equation for synergicity.

It is: W + P = S.

Synergicity, of course, is the *S*.

One solution to the equation, as discussed earlier, is when *W* and *P* represent *work* and *plan*. After all, that seems to be the formula for almost everything in this world. Work for it! Work hard, work long! Strive and strive and work and work until you get it. And work smart by planning—strategize and figure out how you are going to get what you want.

But the equation of work and plan does not bring synergicity, no matter how well you plan or how hard you work. One reason the equation doesn't add up is that synergicity, as we have defined it, is a gift of attitude and of spirit—a heartset rather than something we can earn or buy.

WATCH AND PRAY EQUALS SYNERGICITY

So we return to a frequent theme of this book. The true and accurate formula is *watch and pray*.

To find synergicity we must first learn to truly watch—to see things as they really are. When we notice the spiritual, as well as the physical and mental, and become ever more aware and perceive with ever greater perspective, we begin to see a perfect timing and just the right course to take. We begin to appreciate the connections between all things and to see coincidences not as matters of chance but as manifestations of a divine hand and as opportunities to find and fulfill life's deeper purposes.

And it is by praying or meditating that we can interpret all we see according to a larger vision that enables us to see beyond and go beyond what we could achieve on our own.

We can recognize so many profound differences when we contrast the accepted way of doing things in the world, the work and plan way, with the more spiritual formula—watch and pray. Working and planning is depending on yourself and using your own power of mind and personality to make things happen. It is a good thing—but remember, it is a limited thing. Watching and praying (which can often lead us to rechanneled working and planning) is a spiritual equation which uses synergy with others and synchronicity with the universe to bring ourselves and others to the best place we can be.

For many years, we had a home in Jackson, Wyoming, and kept a riverboat in the garage. It was a flat-bottomed boat made specifically for floating down the Snake River. Though I haven't done it for

several years, I recall vividly the incredible beauty of floating effortlessly through the forests beneath the Grand Tetons.

When I say "effortlessly," that is not quite true. The riverboat had oars which could keep you out of trouble if you were headed toward the center of some rapids or if the river split into channels and you had to get yourself across to the right one.

It was the perfect experiential explanation for the term "rechanneling"—in fact, come to think of it, it may be the actual experience from which the rechanneling metaphor is taken. Often, when we got into a wrong channel, no amount of rowing or paddling or pushing could get you through it, and no matter how hard you worked, you ended up running out of water or the water got too shallow and you had to portage back upstream and "rechannel."

And planning it out on your own before floating was often not enough. The maps didn't show everything and channels have a way of changing.

So we learned to watch and to ask. We learned that if you watched well enough, you could see into which channel the most water was flowing and that was the one to take. And whenever there was another boater to ask, particularly one who had made this channel choice before, that was the surest way to rechannel.

So the work and plan formula and the watch and pray channel are not opposites or enemies—they both need each other. We rechannel our work and our plans by the answers and insights we get through our watching and praying.

The spiritual $W + P = S$ formula can be elaborated and expanded. Consistent with the equation, the W and P can also mean:

Wonder and Perceive

Waiting and Patience

Willing and Petitioning

Worship and Praise

Wander and Ponder

All of the equation alternatives are about sensitive observation, awareness, and perspective—about seeing through our senses and, more importantly, through our hearts and souls. Nudges, impressions, guidance, and inspiration become as important as eyes and ears. The needs of others become as

important as our own. Discovering and working towards our purpose becomes the goal, and the vastness of the universe compared to our nothingness guides our thinking at every unexpected turn. We plan and try to think ahead, but we are watchful—willing—at every juncture to change course and seize unanticipated opportunities and possibilities as they are placed before us.

WATCH

I had an aunt, May Swenson, my mother's sister, who was one of America's greatest and most honored twentieth-century poets. As a small boy, I remember having "watching" experiences with her. "Look at that tree," she would say to me, "and tell me what you see." I would see bark and limbs and leaves. She would say, "Look harder, look closer and tell me what you see." Then she would tell me of the patterns she saw in the bark, the shapes and forms in the canopy, the way the wind had shaped the tree's growth, how the leaves spun clockwise, why the moss was on the north side of the trunk, where the squirrels might have put nuts, which ways the branches seemed to be reaching, and dozens of other things that I had not seen because I was not watching closely or poetically enough.

If there is so much to see just by examining a simple tree, imagine what happens when we use all our senses and develop a mindset and a heartset that opens our spiritual eyes as well. This is where we find the *empathy* and *charity* to appreciate the different perspectives in what other people see.

The more we notice, the more we grow, and our ability to observe and understand what others feel or what they need is enhanced. *This is true empathy.* And the more we notice, the more we connect to people, to nature, to ideas, and to loving and giving. *This is true charity.*

We can train our physical eyes to see more just as my aunt tried to train me. We can develop each of our five senses to take in more, notice more, to be more aware and gain more perspective.

Taking a solitary walk one day through a neighborhood in Southampton, in Southern England, I came upon a blind man with his dog, selling baskets on a street corner. He introduced himself as George and I struck up a conversation. He was delightful, insightful—and funny! When I asked him if he made all the baskets himself, he said, "Well, except for the dog baskets—my dog makes those."

As we talked, he must have perceived some hint of pity in my voice, because he said, suddenly, "Hey, don't feel so bad for me. You have one sense that is better than mine, but I have four senses that are better than yours. I can hear more, smell more, taste more, and feel more than you can!" He then began to demonstrate by telling me things he could hear right then that I could not hear and things he could smell right then that I could not smell. "I've developed my other senses to make up for the eyesight I've lost," he said, "and the best sense of all is what I feel in my heart."

Watching does not refer just to what we see with our eyes. Learn to watch (and be aware) with all of your senses and remember what George learned: It is not with our physical senses that we do our most important watching—it is with our heart. It is with our spiritual eyes and ears through which we can sense the most important things in life.

PRAY

There are probably as many different kinds of meditation and prayer as there are different people. However and whenever you pray, or whatever style of meditation or quiet contemplation you use, there are some basic principles that apply.

When we pray or meditate, do we ask for insight, perspective, awareness; do we ask and ponder on our purpose or how we can help someone who is struggling? Do we express our thoughts and plans and ask for feedback, guidance, and clarity? Do we LISTEN and wait for answers, promptings, and new perceptions? And do we take notes on it so that we can remember answers,

implement them, learn from them, and do what we are prompted to do? I mentioned earlier a remarkable man I worked for who liked to have a prayer prior to important meetings or in connection with important decisions. He was not apologetic about it; in fact, he approached it in an almost utilitarian and practical way. "Why not pray?" he would say, "After all, God knows more about this than we do."

Another friend does something very similar with meditation. He makes a point of arriving five minutes early for appointments and pausing for a moment before making an important call. He envisions how he wants the conversation to unfold and puts himself in the right mood for it. "I get little impressions that make me approach things in a better way," he says, "and I can't tell if they come from inside of me or from outside of me."

Some meditation can happen in an instant. I asked Maria Sharapova, the tennis star, in a press conference why it was that she turned away from the court and stood motionless just for a moment between each point. She answered that she was taught as a junior player to just pause and re-center her mind before each new point in the match.

Alfred Lord Tennyson said, "More things are wrought by prayer than this world dreams of." Prayer is both a way to gain insight and direction and a way to actually influence outcomes.

Prayer and meditation can not only bring things to pass, they can open the channels whereby we see what the divine wants us to see, and whereby we learn to watch with spiritual eyes and discover—all around us—the synergicity that allows us to maximize our lives and the lives of others.

C O M B I N I N G   T H E   P O W E R   O F
W A T C H I N G   A N D   P R A Y I N G

The beauty of the spiritual W + P = S formula is that not only do watching and praying lead to synergicity, they help and enhance each other. In other words, as we move closer and deeper into synergicity, watching leads to better praying and praying leads to better watching.

Those who become truly watchful begin to notice all kinds of things to focus their prayers and contemplations on. They see needs, opportunities, and situations more accurately; they know what help is needed and thus what to ask for and what to do. And, the more they see, the more they have to be thankful for. The thoughts and prayers of a true watcher are expansive and filled with insight and empathy. One tends to search for purpose and to focus on how he or she can serve others, becoming a seeking mechanism, searching for more of what their spirit should perceive.

Those who meditate and pray hard—who exercise their thought and wrestle with the divine in prayer—become much better watchers, because their spiritual eyes are opened. They begin to see more, feel more, and become more aware of others and, thus, more guided in service and more capable of finding and fulfilling their own destinies.

The equation works. The enhanced watching, and the enhanced praying *do* lead to ever greater synergicity, which, to repeat, is: *A state of mind and spirit that acknowledges (indeed, celebrates) one's complete dependency on higher powers and complete interdependency with other people; an attitude and approach that seeks divine purpose and looks for guidance in all things, particularly in the timing and interconnectedness of life events.*

SERVICE AND MAGIC AS ELEMENTS OF SPIRITUAL SYNERGICITY

Synergicity is an attitude that submerges self and elevates others, yet it does not diminish or undercut the importance of each individual. In fact, in acknowledging the interconnectedness of all things and the interdependency of all people, it magnifies the importance of each person to each other person. It also heightens our sense of responsibility toward each other and thus makes us more interested, involved, and in tune with *service.*

When Linda and I speak or lecture to relatively affluent parents, one of the most frequent questions we get is "How do I un-spoil my

kids?" Many children have so much these days and seem to appreciate it so little! Parents wish there was a "quick fix" for kids who are self-centered, wrapped up in themselves and their little world and are uninterested in helping or even knowing about the needs of others. There really is not a quick fix, of course, but the closest thing to it that we have ever found is to involve kids in service. This can range from shoveling a neighbor's driveway to helping at a local soup kitchen or homeless shelter to going on a service expedition. A family can use its vacation to help build a Habitat for Humanity home in a poor area, or do repairs for refugees or elderly in the inner city, or, where finances permit, go to some Third World location and help a village dig a well, build a school, or establish a health clinic.

In this kind of service, kids become more aware, gain a wider perspective, and obtain more synergicity. It also has a profound effect on the parents to spend time in areas different from what they are used to and to see firsthand some of the poverty and disparity that exists in the world as well as the beautiful people and perspectives that are scattered throughout the earth. It is the closest thing we have ever found to a quick fix for kids' perspectives and sense of entitlement and the fastest way for children to gain a greater realization of human interdependence.

It is not necessary to travel to Africa or the Amazon or even to go to homeless shelters or soup kitchens to see needs and offer help. People around us, right now, right where we are at any given moment, have needs. We are all interdependent. Sometimes just noticing that someone looks a little down or confused or worried can give us the opportunity to ask if there is anything we can do. And often just a smile or a greeting or a well-placed complement can turn the day around for another person. Mother Teresa said, "We shall never know all the good that a simple smile can do."

Some people (my wife Linda is one of them) have a gift of empathy. They just know what people need, so service and helping is natural and easy for them. Others (and I include myself in this category) need to develop and cultivate the quality of empathy. We have to do it by looking at other people harder, focusing on them more, trying to watch and pray concerning how they

feel and what they need. Sometimes determining needs is as simple as asking. "How are you feeling?" or "Is there anything I can do for you?"

And there is another kind of asking and thinking that we can do. We can ponder opportunities to serve. We can ask to be more aware of needs that are in front of us every day.

Does the quality of synergicity expand within us when we do more service? Or do we see opportunities for

It is not necessary to travel to Africa or the Amazon or even to go to homeless shelters or soup kitchens to see needs and offer help.

and give more service as we better develop the attitude and paradigm of synergicity? *Both!* They precipitate each other; they are a true chicken-and-egg situation.

Synergicity is a magical quality in many ways. When I talk about magic, I am referring to instances where things somehow seem to supersede the normal laws that we know, where we go beyond our natural ability and get results beyond what we could logically expect. With synergicity, one plus one can equal three or more and things (and their timing) can seem to align as though the whole universe was conspiring to work together for our good. A little more focus on service can add to this magic.

Virtually every faith and every scripture and every religion and every philosophy teach the double-blessing concept of service. When we help others, we help ourselves. When we make others happy, we make ourselves happy. "Cast your bread on the water," scripture says, "and it will come back to you one hundredfold." Somehow, the greatest gifts we can give are magical in that the more we give of them, the more we have left. It is true of love. It is true of joy. It is true of peace and comfort and good cheer.

There is one more gift—one more motivation for service that is so magnificent we can scarcely comprehend it. It is the magic that assures us that "Inasmuch as ye have done it unto the least of these, my brethren, ye have done it unto me" (Matthew 25:40). Imagine the awesome, incomprehensible opportunity to do things for God—to actually give gifts and do service to the divine. We can do so, in tiny repayment for the fact that God has done

everything for us. And we can do so through service. This is not exclusively a Christian principle. All great religions and enduring philosophies contain statements about the service to fellow men being service to God.

It is hard, in the midst of our own problems, to focus on what we can give more than on what we would like to get. It is hard to think about others' needs when our own needs are so obvious and pressing to us. But it is possible and it is a gift we can attain, a talent that we can develop. And it will give us more synergicity and more joy.

There are actually all kinds of magic in synergicity! If we define magic as things that defy natural laws as we know them or as things that our heart and spirit let us depend on even though they don't add up mathematically, then there is magic all around this third rescuer of joy. Why do we get one hundredfold for all that we give? Laws that we know can't explain it, yet our actions can prove it to others and to ourselves.

It is possible to list and categorize the magical elements and ramifications of synergicity:

1. **The magic of synergy:** When we work together with others, recognizing their talents, understanding that they know things we don't (just as we know things they don't), and respecting the stimulation—the idea leap-frogging—that takes place when we brainstorm or think through something with other people, we begin to benefit from a certain type of magic. When we operate synergistically, we always find that the total is greater than the sum of its parts.

2. **The magic of syncronicity:** When we want things when we want them, we are often disappointed and frustrated. On the other hand, when we work and plan—and watch and pray—for good things, but are patient in the timing, we begin to see wisdom and to grow in perspective. We develop patience and empathy and we learn to see the big picture. There is another type of magic in this, as it is revealed to us (usually after the fact) that the way things happened was for the best, and that there were things we

would never have understood if all had not gone as it did and happened in the time that it happened.

3. **The magic of the absence of coincidences:** As suggested earlier, coincidence is the word we use when we do not see or understand the divine influence or connection. Most things happen for a reason, even if the reason is small or hard to notice at the moment. If we are looking for synergicity, and asking ourselves why something might be happening right now, we can sometimes find reasons or at least see opportunities in that moment. There can be purpose in everything, and magic lies in finding that purpose.

4. **The magic of relationships:** When you think of it, almost every relationship is a kind of miracle. In this world of seven billion people, how did you find your partner or your spouse? Or your best friend? And how did you end up with the children you have, each of whom seem to have been meant to come to you? There are so many "needles" that we do actually, improbably, find in "haystacks." Is it just luck or happenstance, or is it a kind of magic?

5. **The magic that certain things do not diminish as they are given away:** Perhaps this is the most magnificent magic of all (and it is the very core of what we are calling synergicity). Some things actually grow and multiply as they are given to others, unlike temporal things, which deplete. If I give you an apple, I have one less apple. It is on spiritual things that the magic works. If I give you love, I have more love left than what I had before I gave it. It is the same with joy. It is the same with peace. It is the same with what Christ called "good cheer." It is the same with what Hindus call "Karma." The magic works with a lot of things actually, things that we don't usually think of as spiritual, but which really are: compliments, optimism, empathy, sympathy, interest. The more we use

up, the more we have left. The more we give to others, the more they give to us.

A world without this kind of magic is mundane and small. It is governed by basic laws and does not draw down or even consider the powers of spirit. But a world with this magic is both a joy and an adventure. We are awed by what we do not understand. We feel divine love through the magic. We become good receivers as well as good givers, and we find the joy that we were sent here to gain.

I got into a conversation with a self-proclaimed skeptic and atheist one day that made me realize something. He was making the point that he didn't believe anything that science couldn't prove. He was a PhD student at Cornell and loved the academic and intellectual atmosphere. He enjoyed the stimulation of discovering new truth and explanations of things. "If something is true, or if something exists," he said, "then we should be able to prove it or demonstrate it or understand it, and if we can't, there is no reason to believe it." What concerned me was the presumptuousness of his logic. Did he really think human brains were the most superior thing and the final judge of what was real? Was he ready to reject anything that he couldn't prove or see or hear? All I could think of to say to him was, "Leave a little room for the possibility of magic—of things you may not be able to understand or explain. The mystery of life is part of what makes it exciting and worth living."

Synergicity is a symbol and a reminder of how small we are, but it is also a way to love and revel in that smallness because of the magical way in which it can connect and combine and collaborate with other people, other ideas, other forces, and other spirits and become part of something that is very powerful and potentially very joyful.

Another part of the magic is that we each become individually more rather than less within this loving, lasting, larger whole.

LIVING THE NEW PARADIGM FOR HAPPINESS

CHAPTER 16

THE WHO, WHEN, WHAT, WHERE, AND WHY OF THE JOY RESCUERS

WHO: IS THIS REALLY FOR YOU?

Who is this book written for?

Well it certainly isn't for everyone.

If you are reasonably satisfied with your life, it's probably not your time. If you feel that you are gaining more and more control of more

and more things and if that pursuit is bringing you more satisfaction than frustration, stay with it.

If you feel like you own just about the right number of things, and if they bring you joy or if you are happy in the pursuit of more, go for it.

And if you always feel self-sufficient—physically, mentally, and emotionally—and believe that independence will always be more appealing to you than interdependence, stay on that course.

The question of *who* is collectively a little complicated, but individually it is simple: whoever has thought about it enough to decide that he or she wants the alternatives more than the deceivers—whoever is fed up enough with the paradox and wants to switch to the paradigm.

WHEN: SEEING THE DECEIVERS AS A LEARNING PHASE

When is the best time to advance from the paradox to the paradigm?

You already know that I think the best answer is "as soon as you possibly can." But understand that this is an advanced paradigm . . . It is a graduate degree in life. Generally it is not something that I would try to teach to life's undergraduates.

Having said that, I am amazed how much the concepts of serendipity, stewardship, and synergicity appeal to the audiences of college students that I speak to. They have an inbred, natural sense of adventure and a relish for the unexpected that makes serendipity attractive to them. Many of them have a distaste for materialism and commercialism that helps them warm to stewardship. And there are always a surprising number who already know and use the words *synergy* and *synchronicity* and are intrigued by welding the words together.

Still, despite the intrigue, most younger adults are not prime candidates for the full paradigm. Most people are more primed for these new approaches after they have pursued control, ownership, and independence long enough to know that it doesn't work and have become open to something higher.

Now that we have dug deeply and explored each of the paradigms of ser-endipity, stewardship, and synergicity, we can revisit control, ownership, and independence as a life phase that can prepare us for the paradigm shift.

Let me elaborate on that a bit as we consider that the answer to *when* may be "After we have passed through and want to go beyond CO&I."

Ironically, much of my time these days is spent with Linda advocating control, ownership, and independence as the very lessons parents should teach their children. Let me explain, because it will allow me to elaborate on what I want you to understand about the progression from these to the mindset and heartset of serendipity, stewardship, and synergicity—the tran-sition from the CO&I to SS&S, from *paradox* to the *paradigm*.

One outgrowth of our books is that we have been on the speaking circuit for as many as one hundred days a year. We present to corpo-rate, school, association, and church groups. Our topics are always about families, parenting, and LifeBalance (balancing work, family, and personal needs). We have done five around-the-world speaking tours and have presented in more than fifty countries with a broad array of different cultures, economies, religions, and political systems. Our audiences have been amazingly diverse. Our topics are usual-ly aimed at parents and those who seek more balance between their work lives and their family and personal priorities. We find that fam-ily is the stated highest priority of almost everyone and that the needs and worries and the hopes and dreams of parents are pretty universal and essentially cut across religious, societal, political, and economic differences. Parents in India or Indonesia or Italy have pretty much the same concerns as parents in Indiana or Illinois or Idaho.

The main thrust of most of our parenting presentations is designed to help parents teach initiative and motivation to their kids, and to help those children to learn how to live responsibly in the world. The most popular of our lectures is called "Raising Responsible Kids and Avoiding the Entitlement Trap."

*Now here's what's interesting, given what you know about me and my life views after reading this book: what we often tell parents is that **ownership** is a prerequisite of responsibility and the job of a*

parent is to help children to become **independent** *and learn to have self-***control**.

How can I tell parents to teach their kids control, ownership, and independence and then turn around and write in this book that these three things are the three joy robbers? Control, ownership, and independence represent a level of life, a level of thinking, and a level of responsibility that have to be learned and experienced if one is to reach the higher levels of serendipity, stewardship, and synergicity. Children need to perceive ownership of things before they will begin to take care of them and feel responsible for them. They must gain a degree of control, particularly of themselves, in order to mature and to accept responsibility for who they are. And children must become progressively more independent of their parents if they are to become capable adults who can live their own lives (preferably at an address different from that of their parents).

Much of what we present or speak about has to do with the right ways and the right timing for turning over more ownership, control, and independence to kids. We tell parents that their ultimate goal is to work themselves out of a job—to get their kids to a point where they feel ownership for their things and for their goals, to where they can control their tempers and their appetites, and to where they can think independently and thus overcome peer pressure and make good decisions.

But then guess what we say next? We tell those same parents that it is time for them (the parents) to understand that the very attitudes of control, ownership, and independence that they need to teach to their children can become a very big problem and a limiting factor for them as adults. We suggest that it is time for them, as grown-ups, to find and live by a higher and more spiritual perspective, to develop a deeper paradigm in which they focus more on their interdependence with other people, on the **stewardships** *they are responsible for and on the development of personal* **serendipity** *and* **synergicity** *so that their lives become more exciting, more full, more interesting, and more inspired!*

So, within the context of this sequence of levels, perhaps calling control, ownership, and independence "the three deceivers" or "the joy robbers" is a little harsh. I call them that because I strongly believe that when they are carried with us too long and too far, and viewed as the ends or the goals of our lives, they deceive us greatly. They limit the joy we can find and undermine the quality of our lives.

I could call CO&I "the three stepping-stones to a higher consciousness" or "the three prerequisites that should be practiced and learned and then discarded in favor of a higher level of living and thinking." But that takes too long to say and just isn't strong enough to convince you to leave them behind when the time comes.

At any rate, the fact is that control, ownership, and independence are useful economic and responsibility-training concepts that people need to learn and practice for *a while* before they are ready to shift to the more accurate and more happiness-bringing paradigm of stewardship and synergicity. A while doesn't have to be a long time and, in the end, you will have to answer the *when* question for yourself.

But if you have read this book to this page, you have the keys to make that shift and the *when* could well be *now*!

WHAT: THE ULTIMATE PARADIGM SHIFT

I have been giving you definitions for the rescuers and all of their components for this whole side of the book, so why pose the question of *what* again? Simply because there is one more answer to the *what* question that may be the most important of all.

The ability to notice and recognize the hand (and guidance and inspiration and nudges—and even the intervention) of a higher power in our everyday lives is the true *what*; and this key lies at the root of the deepest kind of serendipity, stewardship, and synergicity.

I know of a highly accomplished man who made a resolution to make a daily journal entry every time he recognized God's hand that day. He made that kind of entry every day for many years. Imagine how tuned-in he became to God's tender mercies, and to the large and small ways that the divine inputs and intervenes in our lives, and to the fact that "God is in the details."

As I pondered this man, making his journal entry every day, this intellectual giant, blessed with an exceptionally keen mind and heavily involved at the time in the secular and academic worlds as well as the spiritual, I marveled that he could notice things each day that showed him the personal involvement of God in the daily events of his life. I wondered what the entries were like, what type of things he noticed. Were some of them broad and general as he observed the beauty of nature? Or were most of them personal, involving the thoughts that came to his mind or the coincidences that weren't really coincidences, or the people that entered his life to help him or to be helped by him.

Whatever the case, it is clear that looking for the divine in our everyday lives is a marvelous key to raising our paradigm to a happier and more spiritual level and allows us to begin to see the world in soulful vision rather than in worldly vision. And the simple exercise of looking, daily, for a divine hand and then recording it in a journal is one simple and elegant way to do it.

The happiness paradigm, ultimately, is a heartset more than a mindset. It is setting our hearts on being part of something higher and desiring to be linked to the biggest *what* of all.

WHERE: IN, AND YET OUT OF, THE WORLD

It all begins, I believe, in a place called gratitude.

Over this past year, as I have been writing about the three deceivers and their three alternatives, I have realized that the deceivers minimize gratitude, while the alternatives of serendipity, stewardship, and synergicity

maximize gratitude. As attitudes and life-approaches, they are spawned by thankfulness and produce gratitude. And with these attitudes certain things begin to happen:

- When we live in this place we focus on the real, the most important, the most lasting parts of life. Our relationships, our growth, and how we impact the world and those around us become our measuring sticks. We still live in this frantic, frenetic world, but we are free from trying to be or do what everyone else is or does.
- We are *in* the world! We are involved. We love life. We find joy in this world's endless beauty and diversity, and even in its challenges and hardships. Loving others and not judging them allows us to serve with joy. Knowing what is going on, and developing a breadth of widespread interests, invigorates our minds. We appreciate life with all of its variety and magnificent options.
- Within this *in*-but-not-*of* place, we do not try to emulate everything *of* the world! We focus on long-lasting goals, not the latest fad or fashion. We set goals and live our lives based on more spiritual perceptions. Feeling confident in our own opinions, interests, and ideas allows us to be open to inspiration and real joy.

Consider three keys to unlock this *in*-but-not-*of* door:

1. *Train yourself,* your family, and those around you to strive to influence more than they are influenced. If we live our life in protective mode—always trying to avoid everything that could be bad or that might pull us away from our comfort zone—we are acting like pawns on the chessboard, not kings or queens.
2. *Remember* that it is our attitudes that determine how interested we are in the world, and it is also our attitudes that determine how well we can keep ourselves from

becoming slaves to the world and to its fashions. There are wonderful things here; we should focus on those that bring joy and help us share that joy with others. If our paradigms and perceptions revolve around serendipity, stewardship, and synergicity then we will see the world and find its joys more realistically.

3. *Understand* you are both a physical being and a spirit or soul. Somewhere between your spirit and your body is your brain—somewhere between because both your body and your spirit use your brain. Your body uses it for everything from coordinating your breathing and walking to doing math problems. Your spirit uses your brain to take in and interpret sensory and physical data and to allow the spiritual you to interphase and interact with this world. So, your brain is a tool of your spirit, but it is also a tool of your body. The real question is: Which one (your spirit or your body) has the predominate and ultimate control of your brain? Which of the two does your brain serve and have the most allegiance to? If your brain is most closely aligned with your body, with the physical world, and with the lusts and materialism and consumerism of modern society, then you will be in the world *and* an indiscriminate partaker of all the world offers. But if your brain is most closely aligned with your spirit, with the humility of faith and belief and the more forward-thinking perspective, then you will be in the world but not *of* the world. And it is this juxtaposition that brings happiness.

The beauty of it is that we can shape the way we think and construct and determine our attitudes. We can balance our body and our spirit as we make decisions. We can do this by adopting the perspective of stewardship and understanding we are caretakers of our body, mind, and spirit. We can do it by taking on the paradigm of serendipity and looking for and welcoming guidance and the unexpected. And we can do it by living with synergicity

and enjoying our interdependence with others and the blessings of divine timing. We can notice that our life unfolds in beautiful ways we would never have imagined on our own.

The answer to *where* is the double helix of in and not of.

WHY: FOR WHAT IT GIVES TO YOU AND FOR WHAT IT GIVES TO OTHERS THROUGH YOU

Reasons for making the switch from the robbers to the rescuers have been part of almost every page of this book, but let me answer the *why* question even more personally:

What I love about the alternative attitudes of serendipity, stewardship, and synergicity is that they each:

1. Emphasize and draw our attention to the spiritual.
2. Deepen our humility by giving us the perspective of our very small place in a very big universe.
3. Develop within us an upward spiritual spiral of empathy and charity, relying more on "watch and pray" than on "work and plan."
4. Make us free to live an authentic life.
5. Lower our stress, pressure, and tension because we depend less on ourselves and more on others, including the divine. Instead of pressure they give us PEACE.
6. Put greater focus on others and allow us to be a more transparent self, which enables us to LOVE more.
7. Give us more of the moments and the gratitude and the excitement that equates to more JOY.

A final *why* that has not been mentioned enough is resilience.

We live in a world where the ability to bounce back is critical. Setbacks

and failures happen more frequently and are more exposed to others than ever before.

The deceivers spotlight and magnify the knock-downs of our lives—and in our minds. Everything we can't control or don't own, and even everything we have to admit that we need, undermines our self status and can edge us toward discouragement and depression. We can fight these and gain some temporary victories, but in the long range we lose, because at their very foundations, the deceivers will always allude us and eventually prove themselves to be lies.

Resilience and the ability to bounce back from failure or falling short is closely tied to our attitude . . . Serendipity teaches us to look for something better than the thing we were seeking but didn't reach . . . Stewardship reminds us that whatever it is, is not ours anyway and all we can do is our best . . . and Synergicity reassures us that we can always get more help and try again and that the timing may be better later.

With the SS&S paradigm we don't drop as far and we bounce back up faster. We are rescued.

So, a last answer to the *why* is *resilience.*

———

CHAPTER 17

THE HOW: DAILY EXERCISES FOR SERENDIPITY, STEWARDSHIP, AND SYNERGICITY

Who, when, what, where, and why are interesting questions, but it is the how question that can reorient your life.

It's one thing to talk about serendipity, stewardship, and synergicity and how adopting them as attitudes can help us and make us happier. But it's another thing to actually acquire the habits and attitudes of the rescuers—to really incorporate them into our lives and minds and hearts. It takes time and effort to make SS&S the paradigms within which we live our lives.

Developing new attitudes is very much like developing new muscles. It takes exercise! This chapter will introduce you to some mental planning and recording exercises designed to help you notice new things and to develop and build more serendipity, stewardship, and synergicity into your life!

To develop mental, emotional, and spiritual muscle, the exercises are of greatest value when done daily.

To develop mental, emotional, and spiritual muscle, the exercises are of greatest value when done daily. Like any exercise, whatever you can manage to do is far better than nothing! I know of people who receive a lot of benefits and make measurable progress from implementing suggestions like those in this chapter even very haphazardly and inconsistently—but of course, it is good to be as consistent as possible. If we are going to change the paradigms or the lenses through which we view the world and the very attitudes that we carry around with us every day, we will need well-conceived exercises that alter the way we think and expand our awareness and perspective.

As I worked to implement serendipity, stewardship, and synergicity more fully, I learned that it was far easier to understand the way you want to perceive and approach life than to actually change the attitudes and thought patterns. I needed to find specific ways to implement and apply the rescuers every day. New habits are hard to form, and new paradigms are even harder. There came a point when I realized that part of the difficulty was the planners and time-management tools and scheduling apps that I was using. They were all essentially designed to facilitate more control, more ownership, and more independence, they were about segmenting your life, setting priorities, and making and checking off lists. The typical apps and planners led me and my thought processes away from observation, empathy, and reflection. I tried to adjust the way I planned my day, but the tools were working against me, so I developed a new type of daily overview that moved my mind in opposite directions. I call it "The Anti-Planner." Its three daily elements are the *Serendipity Line*, the *Stewardship Blanks*, and the *Synergicity Bands*.

These daily elements facilitate daily exercises for increasing your happiness. None of them require a lot of time, but all require commitment, effort, focus, and concentration. After all, what we are trying to change is how we see the world around us and how we respond and live our lives day to day.

The three exercises involve writing in a daily journal or planner. The writing you will be asked to do is not extensive—in fact, it is just a few words each day, but those words are important. They allow you to record the results of the exercises, to check yourself, and work toward consistency in the habits you are trying to develop.

MONDAY

While many do their calendars and their schedules on their smartphones, please do these exercises first on paper—either in an old-fashioned paper planner or just in a nice portable notebook. Once you have learned the principles and practices of the exercises, you can implement their principles in your phone calendar or in any electronic planning method.

THE SERENDIPITY LINE

Think for a moment about how we usually plan our day and try to carry out that plan: we often write down our meetings or appointments and make lists of things to do. It's a helpful process because it keeps us from forgetting commitments and helps us remember the needs of the day and prioritize what we want to get accomplished.

But here's the problem: the day never goes as we planned. Things come up, people we need to contact aren't available, we get interrupted, things happen that we couldn't have anticipated. All these unpredictables throw our plans off and often frustrate us. We want control; we think control is what we should be seeking. We know we can't control everything around us, but at least we want to control our day, our schedule, and what we accomplish. When new and unexpected needs come up, we sometimes feel that the whole world is conspiring against our plan for the day. There must be a way to pursue our lists and our goals *and* find serendipity along the way.

To allow for planning with a heart open for life's twists and turns, I developed what I call the *Serendipity Line*. This was introduced as we discussed serendipity earlier. Here is more on how to implement this magically simple tool:

In your daily planner, a journal, or just a simple notebook, draw a vertical line down through the middle of the page. Put your plans and meetings and appointments and activities on the left side of the page. On the right side, write down the serendipities that come to you that day (the unplanned things, the gifts).

Basically the left side (which can represent the left hemisphere of your brain, the analytical, logical side) is the way you want the day to go. It is your

best effort to organize what you plan to do. It is written in terms of what you will do in your immediate future: go to the meeting, write the memo, pick up the kids. It is your to-do list.

The right half of the page (which can represent the right hemisphere of your brain, the creative, intuitive side) starts out blank, except for the heading of "Serendipities." What you write here as the day goes by, or at the end of the day looking back, will be in the past tense, because serendipities can't be planned; your right-side notes will tell of moments that actually happened. They will be things like an unexpected call from an old friend or a beautiful sunset that you took a minute to watch and appreciate. Something you noticed, a new person you met, a little spontaneous thing you did, a complement someone gave you: "watched an exceptional sunset," "got a surprise call from my cousin," "got an idea while showering."

Your serendipities will not all be pleasant. They are simply what is—what happens as we go about our plans but see other opportunities and even challenges. They could include unwelcome surprises that you made the most of. A traffic jam that gave you the chance to listen to music, a meeting that went overtime but where you noticed an opportunity, someone who was late that gave you time to call your mother, a sickness that helped you appreciate health.

Noticing and discovering serendipities is a learned skill. It is something we can become better and better at. It is, as the definition suggests, a "state of mind."

For the first few days, serendipities may be hard to spot or recognize, but as you become more aware, as you notice more and as you watch for the unexpected, unplanned, and unplannable things, your ability to recognize serendipities will increase. And as you seek guidance, your serendipities will take on a more inspirational, more spiritually guided tone.

Noticing and discovering serendipities is a learned skill. It is something we can become better and better at. It is, as the definition suggests, a "state of

mind" involving awareness and sensitivity to what is around us. I challenge you, for starters, to find at least three serendipities each day and to write them down on the right side of each day's page. As you do this, you will think more and more in terms of serendipity and less and less in terms of control. The result will be less frustration and more excitement and adventure in your life.

Remember our definition of serendipity: a state of mind, whereby a person, through awareness and sensitivity, frequently finds something better than that which he was seeking.

Looking for serendipities and jotting them down on the right side of the serendipity line is a way of training yourself to be more aware, more sensitive, and to watch for the little surprises and perspectives, the opportunities and ideas, and the beauties that can make life a fun ride. Serendipity is an acquired skill, a developed attitude. Having a conscious goal to recognize and write down at least three or four each day will help you gain the skill and learn the attitude.

As you do, the unexpected, uncontrollable things that happen each day, the ones that used to be viewed as interruptions, irritations, and impediments, will start to look more like opportunities, surprises, and tender mercies.

At the end of a week, go back through your daily pages and evaluate the left and right sides. You will find that the value of the serendipities on the right rivals that of the planned and executed accomplishments on the left.

Start implementing the serendipity line tomorrow. It will make your life more exciting, but also calmer and more accepting. Most importantly, it will lead you to a place where you are more receptive to beauty, to surprise, to hunches and intuition, and to gratitude and guidance.

THE STEWARDSHIP BLANKS

Most of us have many *have-to-dos* in each day. They are the things we put on our to-do list on the left side of our page (drop off the kids, make the phone calls, write the memo, mow the lawn, schedule fundraiser, etc.). They are the things we do at work or at home or in our free time. Sometimes the

MONDAY

have-to-dos consume our entire day and the urgent takes over and pushes aside the more important things like reading a story to the kids, spending a quiet moment with your spouse, or taking the time to exercise or meditate. The *Stewardship Blanks* are designed to prevent this. Here is what you do:

At the top of your planner or daily journal, put three short horizontal lines. These are called Stewardship Blanks and they are the *choose-to-dos* of life. They need to take priority over and have a working balance with the have-to-dos. Fill them in *before* you start listing appointments or duties or commitments.

On the first line, write one thing that you choose to do that day for your family. Not something someone is expecting you to do, like picking up the

kids or fixing dinner. Something you *choose* to do because you ask yourself, "What does someone in my family really need today?" On the second line, write one thing you choose to do for your work or community. Again, this is not something you are expected to do, like fill out the report or conduct the meeting. It is something need-based, such as: "write a thank you note to Jennifer who helped me with the layout of the sales report" or "volunteer at the girls' club downtown" or "visit Mary who just went through a loss." It is usually something people-oriented, something you decide because you ask yourself, "What does someone need?" On the third line, write one thing you choose to do for yourself. What is something *you* need that day in order to feel better, to refresh yourself, or to grow or learn in some way. It might be exercise, reading scripture, or meditating. It may be practicing a new skill or learning about something that interests you. It will be something you do not have to do or that others are expecting you to do. It will be something you choose to do for yourself.

Your three greatest stewardships each day are your family, your work or community, and yourself. If you do one choose-to-do for each of them each day, and if you prioritize that choose-to-do above any of the have-to-dos, your life will begin to orient itself more to stewardship. The three choose-to-do enhance each other and form a priority triangle that can stabilize your life. The top corner ($\bigwedge$) is yourself, the right corner ($\searrow$) is your family, and the left corner ($\diagdown$) is work and community.

A certain magic happens when we train ourselves through this daily exercise to think of our stewardships—our choose-to-dos—our real priorities *first*, before we make the list of have to dos. The magic is that we somehow still find time for the have-to-dos. The have-to-dos, when they are listed first, seem to crowd out even the thought of any choose-to-dos. "Too busy today," we think as we look at our list, "maybe tomorrow I will find time for my family and for myself." Magically though, when we list the choose-to-dos first, they don't get in the way of the have-to-dos.

This phenomenon is difficult to explain, except perhaps with an analogy. If you take a jar and fill it with sand, there will be no room for the three larger rocks you also want to put in the jar. But if you put the three rocks in first, you can still pour all the sand in, because it fills in around the three big

rocks. Our days can (and will) work the same. If we think stewardship first, if we write down our three choose-to-dos, we will find they really don't take that long and the have-to-dos will get done at least as well as they would have otherwise.

Try putting your three choose-to-dos at the top of your planning page for the next seven days. Don't list a single thing to do or have-to-do until you have thought for a few minutes about, first, what your family needs; second, what the needs are at your work or in your community; and third, what you need that day. Write down a daily choose-to-do for each. Prioritize those three choose-to-dos. Make them happen each day, even if you don't get everything on your to-do list done. Define your own successful day not by how many things you check off of your longer list, but by whether you thought carefully about the needs of your stewardships and whether you did at least one small but meaningful thing for each.

When the week is over, look back over the past seven days. Ask yourself what was the most important (and most joyful) part of each day.

I'm betting it will be the things you wrote on your three stewardship blanks!

THE SYNERGICITY BANDS

Remember the expanded definition of synergicity:

Synergicity: A state of mind and spirit that acknowledges (indeed, celebrates) one's complete dependency on higher powers and complete interdependency with other people; an attitude and approach that seeks divine purpose and looks for guidance in all things, particularly in the timing and interconnectedness of life events.

The question, of course, is how. How to get into that kind of habit and that kind of thinking? How to change our minds so that they work on a more spiritual plane?

The *Synergicity Bands* exercise is a way to discipline yourself to ask for and look for insight and inspiration three times each day.

Put three Synergicity Bands across your planner, notebook, or daily diary page by simply drawing three thick, horizontal, highlighted lines across your page. (Use a thick yellow highlighter that you can see through or write over.) Put one band at the very top, one at the very bottom, and one in the middle of your daily page. Think of these as the three times to briefly meditate or to pray and to ponder the manifestation of a higher power in your life. Also, think for a minute at those three times—morning, noon, and night—about others you have interacted with, made friends with, done something for, or felt appreciation toward. Jot down (in the Synergicity Bands) any expression

of God's hand, recognitions of something greater than what you could do on your own, or any meaningful interaction with another person.

This is, of course, simply a way to make us more aware of our dependence on the divine or a higher power and of the little answers or inspirations or beauty that come to us every day. When

To see spiritual influence in our lives gets easier and easier as we watch for it, notice it, and write it down.

we don't see them, it is not because they are not there; it is because we fail to notice them. To see spiritual influence in our lives gets easier and easier as we watch for it, notice it, and write it down. The beauty of needing other people, learning from them, and benefiting from their gifts, and vice versa, is the blessing of knowing we are interdependent and that we all have the capacity to help and to love others.

Keep track of these little moments of light and understanding. Write instances that show our interdependence on others. Think about these briefly three times a day. This spiritual exercise will bring deep joy as we acknowledge where we fit into this world and into humanity as a whole.

Implementing this habit involves two substantial challenges:

First, you must remember to meditate or pray three times each day. For many, an evening prayer or meditation is a ritual and happens consistently. But praying in the morning, in the commotion of getting up and meeting commitments, is sometimes difficult to remember, and meditation in the middle of the day often does not happen unless we are trying to develop this habit. Let the Synergicity Bands be reminders to take a moment three times each day.

Second, you have to look hard for both the large and small blessings that come into play in your daily life. Since we are dependent on God or nature for all—for every breath, for every aspect of life—it should be easy to notice these seemingly ordinary, though sometimes unexpected, blessings. But most of us are not in the habit of thinking this way or of trying to notice

them. The Synergicity Bands are there to remind us to look and to notice and to acknowledge three times each day.

Often these two challenges will work together. As you pray or meditate, you will become aware of a blessing or an answer or a prompting and you can write it in that morning band. And often, as you see something that reminds you of your blessings, whether it is a beautiful sunset or a simple smile from a friend, it will prompt you to a brief moment of thanks, even as you write it in your Synergicity Band.

PUTTING THE THREE
DAILY HABITS TOGETHER

A blank daily planning page that incorporates the habits for all three of the three joy-rescuing paradigms looks like this.

I subscribe to the theory that when you do something for twenty-one straight days, it then deserves to be called a habit. Fill in the three Stewardship Blanks each morning before you do or even think about anything else. During the day, pause briefly to meditate or pray three times—first thing as you wake, midday or as you transition from work to home, and last thing before you sleep—and write down the pause-and-ponder thoughts that come to you in the three Synergicity Bands. And all through the day, watch for and write down the serendipities that come to you on the past-tense, right side of the Serendipity Line.

Here is a two-pronged promise: First, at the end of the twenty-one days these exercises will have become more than exercises—they will be the best habit you have ever formed. Second, as you look back over those twenty-one days, you will find that what you have written in the Stewardship Blanks, in the Synergicity Bands, and on the right side of the Serendipity Line will be of more value than the total of everything else you have done during those twenty-one days.

THE ULTIMATE METHOD OF PURSUIT

We have spent this chapter outlining ways to change our minds and flip our paradigms. The techniques of the Serendipity Line, the Stewardship Blanks, and the Synergicity Bands are guaranteed habit-formers that can be very helpful in this regard. They can begin to change the way we see, the way we think, and the way we understand.

Still, techniques and methods are of limited value when we are dealing with things of the spirit. A more spiritual perspective and paradigm cannot be completely developed by mental means or physical habits. This is not to

say that our own efforts don't count. Self-help, particularly when it centers on truths, can be truly transforming.

One of the hallmarks of our ability to make choices is that we can, to a large extent, decide who we will be and then move closer to that ideal by our will and our determination. How we think matters. What we think matters. Who we think we are and who we think we want to be matters. This book, from start to finish, has been written in an attempt to change, in some limited but very important ways, how we think. We are the ones who must do the changing.

But where self-help runs into trouble is when it fails to recognize its limitations. When we depend too much, and too ultimately, on ourselves, we forget how small and limited we are and lose the very humility that would allow us to tap into a higher source.

In the middle of my personal transition from the deceivers to their alternatives, I had developed the Anti-Planner and the methodologies outlined in this chapter, and I thought that now I would move steadily and smoothly into a new set of daily habits and an ever-more-complete revision of my paradigm—or how I see the world and how I operate within it. I was moving from paradox to paradigm, and I was monitoring my serendipity, measuring my stewardships, and checking off my synergistic insights.

Then one day a disturbing thing occurred to me: I was still using the tools of the paradox to build the paradigm. I was taking a control approach to the development of serendipity, stewardship, and synergicity. I was using independent methods and controlled self-reliance to earn the ownership of the rescuer attitudes.

While there was nothing wrong with making a conscious effort to kick certain habits and attitudes and shift to better ones, the underlying idea that I could do it by myself and then come to own and control it was contrary to the whole premise.

I altered my course in a simple way: I kept trying and working at it, but reminded myself frequently and consciously that I couldn't do it by myself and needed help from the very higher source I was trying to tie into. I began to pray and meditate in a new and humbler way

and to acknowledge that the serendipity, stewardship, and synergicity
I wanted ultimately had to come from somewhere higher than myself.

GIFTS

We can change our minds, but it takes something deeper, more spiritu-al, to change our hearts and to change our souls. A greater calmness and tranquility, and a more ordered and accurate thinking, can be developed and brought about through mental exercises. But there is something greater, something beyond the calm and clarity that we can bring about in ourselves. It is the gift of peace and the light of inspiration that comes not from within us but from without and above us, from the source of light and peace and truth. It is not earned or deserved or won. It is received as a gift by those who ask.

There are two very good things that come from working and striving for (and adopting habits that lead to) the attitudes of serendipity, steward-ship, and synergicity. The first good thing is that, as we strive, we begin to develop these new ways of looking at the world and we begin to escape from the deceptions that are their op-posites. The second good thing that comes from striving for these qualities is that we put ourselves in a position to ask for them. Our actions, as in any aspect of life, enhance and enliven our faith. We are more likely to receive a gift that we are already working toward.

So, the final and ultimate method we should all adopt in our quest for serendipity, stewardship, and synergicity, is a simple three-worder: *ask for them.*

You know by now that these three *S* words are just symbols and attitude changes that represent spiritual concepts. *Serendipity* is another way of

saying faith and guidance and acceptance of life's purposes. *Stewardship* incorporates humility, empathy, charity, and diligence. And *synergicity* really means a meek recognition of our complete interdependence, the often unexplainable timing of life, and seeing the beauty and the divine all around us.

The names or symbols of serendipity, stewardship, and synergicity, as well as the paradigm they lead us to, give us good transitions out of worldly views and into deeper spiritual vision. They are bridge words that do not pit the world against the spirit, but rather try to integrate them. They are paradigms that allow us to have the attitude of living in this amazing world, while not choosing to live like everyone around us.

Ask in prayer and meditation that you might gradually let go of the notions of control, ownership, and independence, and that you might instead be able to adopt serendipity, stewardship, and synergicity. Use the three daily exercises and allow guidance of spirit and heart to understand and develop these attitudes and ways of living. This daily focus will cause you to think more about and be more aware of the three joy rescuers so that you can seek them as well as ask for them, and notice them as well as receive them, when they enter your life. A calmness of mind and deepening joy and happiness will be the result.

POSTSCRIPT

THE THREE ALTERNATIVES PRAYER

WRITTEN PRAYERS OR MEDITATIONS

come from a religious tradition that does not use written prayers. I believe that our prayers should be personal and spontaneous and from our hearts, and I'm not attracted to the repetitions of reading prayers that someone else has written.

Yet, there is certainly nothing wrong with trying to compose our thoughts, leading to more coherent and more substantive and thoughtful prayer. What I am going to suggest here is not a prayer that anyone should read to God, but rather should use as a guideline for asking for divine help in seeking the right things and in avoiding the deception of the attitudes of the world that can separate us from the Spirit. What I hope will happen is that this prayer

may suggest to your mind some ways in which the new paradigm of the three alternatives can be pursued and asked for.

Think of it, therefore, not as an actual prayer, but as a new-form summary of what the three deceivers and the three alternatives are all about.

And if meditation is more within your comfort zone than prayer, try the guided meditation that follows the prayer. Use it as a reflection and a prompter of further thought.

Because I am a Christian, I have written the prayer in a Christian vernacular. You can transpose it into the wording and form of your own faith tradition.

THE THREE ALTERNATIVES PRAYER

I am thankful, God, to live on this earth in these remarkable, defining days, when options and opportunities are so plentiful, and when truth is easier to find than ever before if we know where to look and can discern it from its distractions and deceivers. I am grateful for the diversity of this, thy earth, and for the richness of experience and perspective that is made possible by this mortality which You have designed.

I thank You for the relative freedom that exists and for the agency that allows me to choose how I will think, how I will live, and how I will worship. I thank You for the guidelines and for the true answers that are available to one who seeks and who is faithful and committed.

I thank You for all the stewardships You have given me, for this physical body and all that goes with it, for the choices I can make to shape my life, for my family and the promise of eternity with those I love most, for gifts and talents—both those I have found and developed to a degree and those I am yet seeking. I thank You for the guidance available through Your Spirit and for Your great plan of happiness into which my spirit and destiny can fit. I thank You for my dependence on You in every respect, even for the air I breathe and for my interdependence on others, particularly with those I love most.

My gratitude overflows for the overwhelming privilege of living in this world, but I pray that I may not become of this world. I acknowledge

that with agency comes risk and the danger of deception, and I recognize the danger that false gods can so easily become our obsessions and addictions and that evil can use the very worldliness of this world to steer us onto wrong or deceptive paths. I ask You to protect me and my family from these deceivers, to help me to recognize them and steer my life away from them and toward Your way and Your will.

I understand that one purpose of life on this planet is to exercise the agency and choice You have given us, to learn to stand for what we believe, and to care for what You have given us. Help me to do it for Your glory and to rise to the higher perspective of seeing things through the lens of my dependence and interdependence and Your will.

Please help me to set righteous goals for my progress in life, but protect me from the pride of thinking I can control or dictate very much of what goes on around me. It is Your will I want to fulfill, not my wants. Please protect me from the narrowness and the blinders of focusing only on my own agenda, and help me to see the needs of others and the bigger picture of Your perspective.

I ask You for guidance, for insight as to what You would have me do, and for promptings and nudges and inspiration from Your Spirit when there is something I should notice, someone I should help, or some small part of my destiny that I might fulfill. Grant to me, God, glimpses of who You want me to be and what You would have me do. Help me please to see the joy of the moment, to appreciate the marvelous journey of mortality and to love all of its unexpected twists and turns, looking in each for ways to serve, for insight, and for beauty.

Please inspire me as I set goals and please give me confirmation on the choices and decisions I reach thoughtfully, but help me to see my objectives as an effort to serve and fit into Your larger plans, and thus to move flexibly to other paths or directions as Your Spirit opens them to me. Help me to grow toward a highly aware, highly in-tune serendipitous attitude that allows me to notice unexpected opportunities to grow, to give, and to conform to the joy of Thy will.

I ask You for protection from the pride and the false notion of ownership, and I acknowledge that You are the owner of all; indeed that You own me through the ransom of Your Son. I am privileged and blessed

to be a steward and grateful for the stewardships You have given me. Help me, to magnify these stewardships, be they talents, be they callings, or be they material things that You have entrusted to me. Help me to take no pride in any of thy gifts or stewardships and indeed to use them for Your glory and to bless others.

Help me to see trials and challenges as other forms of stewardship and to meet them with thy help just as I meet the stewardships of joy. I ask You to use me as an instrument, albeit a small and insignificant one, in Your service, and I ask only for those stewardships that would help me to serve You. As I rid myself of the deception of ownership, help me also to shed the jealousy and envy and covetousness that goes with this deceiver, as well as the condescension and self-satisfaction. I thank You for the simple and emancipating recognition of my own nothingness and of Your everythingness and ask You for the greater love that comes with this attitude of spiritual stewardship.

Protect me also, from the foolish and selfish pride of independence. I acknowledge without reservation my total dependence on You and my complete interdependence with those around me. I trust Your timing and Your power and am so grateful that I do not have to rely on my own. I ask that I can learn from the perspective of others as well as from Your Spirit and never have to rely on my own incredibly limited capacity.

Help me, please, to use the mind You have given me to see needs, connections, and opportunities. Open doors and channels and relationships that allow me to work in synergy with others to bring about good things and to give me the patience and the perspective to appreciate Your timetable and sequences rather than trying to demand my own. Help me to be both a better giver and a better receiver and thus to love more. Guide me in developing a humble and highly aware and appreciative attitude of spiritual synergicity that depends on You, trusts Your timing, and works in harmony with others for the greater good.

I acknowledge You in all, I thank You for all, I trust You in all dear God in Heaven, and ask You for the faith, the hope, and the charity

that I believe are the celestial extensions of what I have pled for in
this prayer.
Amen.

THE THREE ALTERNATIVES MEDITATION

Michele Robbins, my editor for this book, felt that it was important to add a meditation as an alternative to the summary of the prayer—for those who may be non-prayers but who none-the-less appreciate the spiritual component of the SS&S paradigm.

So . . . I invited Michele to write it. And she invites you to join in this little journey whether you regularly practice prayer or meditation, or really haven't experienced either . . . yet. Here is her meditation:

This meditation is designed to be read by a partner or recorded and then played back as you immerse yourself in this journey. Alternatively, you may want to read parts and then meditate section by section. Plan for the meditation to take about ten minutes depending on how much preparation time you like to take at the start and how much relaxation time you use as you come out of the meditation. Let's begin:

Prepare for a journey of positive change. Begin by sitting or lying down. Take a few moments to get comfortable. Feel the ground or chair beneath you as you relax into its supporting structure.

Close your eyes as you imagine descending a small, grassy hill. Take a step as you breath evenly in and then out. Another step is another inhalation and exhalation. Continue with deep breaths, stepping down the hill into a valley: ten, nine; another step takes you to eight and then another to seven; continue stepping gently though the green grass six, five, four. Notice the billowing clouds as you step down toward the bottom of the hill three, two, one.

You are now in a brilliant meadow. As you look around at the yellow and blue flowers, you are encompassed with a feeling of complete

gratitude. Picture in your mind the blessings that bring you joy: your free-doms, family, relationships, talents, opportunities for learning. Feel the impact of your blessings on your daily life and feel thanks as you continue breathing deeply.

Now move your attention to the sounds in the meadow. As you contin-ue walking you can hear your own steps in the grass as the sound of your breathing is joined by the gentle wind and mountain sounds of birds and forest creatures. As you listen more closely you hear the sound of moving water and see a stream nearby. You move toward the stream, attracted to its flowing, life-giving power.

You notice a squirrel carrying a nut to the water and realize that you, too, carry something—a simple pack on your back. But it feels heavier than it should. You stop by the running water, remove your backpack, and pull out a brick that has the word "Control" carved on it; you sense this is a part of your life, a heavy part, that you no longer need. You understand that you cannot control your life any more than you can control the stream, so you set that brick to the side. As soon as you do so you notice something better, an apple tree just ahead of you. So you move toward it thinking of the sweet fruit that will satisfy your hunger. As you eat an apple you understand that you have traded the idea of control for something sweeter and more reward-ing. You embrace the idea of *serendipity* and begin to see serendipities all around you as you place another apple in your pack to remind you of the sweet change you are embracing. As the rivulets from the stream find their way out to water the meadow, you know you will find your way, too. You begin to understand your purpose and feel confident in your ability to prog-ress. You sense the need to travel onward with a plan that is flexible enough to allow you to learn more in your journey from unexpected opportunities that will come.

As you follow the stream, you find that it empties into a little pond. You stop again because your pack still feels heavy. As you peek inside you find another brick with "Ownership" etched deeply into one side. You ponder why you are carrying this brick on your walk. There is really nothing you can own here by this beautiful pond. All you can do is watch the pond car-ing for the clear water and flowers. With a lighter heart you set this brick on

the bank and fill your lungs and your mind with a deep breath of watchful, grateful *stewardship* and wish to share the beauty of the pond with others who you love. You think of other stewardships in your life—of the people and the things that you love—and realize they are all gifts, unearned, like the pond. You soon feel it is time again to move on, so you place a light and delicate flower plucked from the edge of the pond in your bag to remind you of your promise to watch over those things placed in your care. You follow the stream as it spills out the other side of the pond.

The stream is soon joined by another stream. A river is formed. It grows larger and moves at a faster pace—full of energy. You must pick your way down a hill more carefully and pause to check what is making your pack feel heavy. As you reach in you find a final brick, this time with "Independence" carved into its face. You look at the strength and power of the confluent river and feel a desire to put aside independence for the greater energy of synergy, and you decide to be ready to take an interdependent approach to life, open to ideas and talents of the many people in your life. Your heart opens as you feel love for others and the opportunity to grow in your capacity to make a difference for good. You study the river and see that it moves in perfect timing over rocks and around eddies always finding a way to flow forward, and you combine this synchronicity with the synergy and feel a longing for *synergicity*. You place a small smooth rock in your pack to remind you of the perfect timing and unity of the water as it combines and smooths and refreshes all it touches.

As you continue following the river, you hear the water getting louder and you soon approach a small waterfall. Its beauty as it tumbles onward with purpose is inspiring. Its power as it sprays the rocks and grasses all around gives life and vibrance to all it touches. You sit by the falling water and just listen to the gentle roar. You feel the energy and power of serendipity, stewardship, and synergicity, and you take a moment to commit yourself to exploring how to use these attitudes in your life to bless all those around you.

As the sun sinks lower in the sky, you realize you have traveled many miles. Still you feel fresh and strong. You eat the apple from your backpack and plant its seeds in the hopes of a new tree growing where other travelers

may discover its sweetness. You blow the parachute seeds from the flower so more can grow, and you pile the smooth stone atop other smooth stones to mark the way.

You take a moment more to just breathe deeply in and out, counting back up: one, two, three, four, five, six, seven, eight, nine, ten. You are now ready to slowly open your eyes and feel your chair or mat beneath you. You gradually sit up, open and close your hands a few times, wiggle your toes, and end your meditation with three more quiet breaths. In and out; in and out; in and out. You are ready now to go about the rest of your day invigorated and ready to follow your new paradigm for happiness.

AFTERWORD:
ADVANCED SS&S
TRAINING

C hanging your core attitudes and approaches—making the fundamental shift from the paradox of CO&I to the paradigm of SS&S—is
a major undertaking that will have ramifications in every part of
your life. If you are still reading, still with me to the end of this book, I will
assume that you are attracted enough to SS&S that you want to make this
fundamental paradigm shift, or at least move toward it.

For some, this book will be enough. You will adjust and evolve and find
your own way to move from the three deceivers to the three alternatives—
quickly or gradually—in your own individual way and with your own
initiative.

Others may want additional help and training beyond this book—going
deeper, delving into case studies, getting the coaching and guidance to apply
SS&S to everything. Because it *can* apply to everything.

There is SS&S eating,
SS&S driving,
SS&S communicating,
SS&S goal-setting,

SS&S parenting,
SS&S marriage,
SS&S vacationing.
SS&S gratitude,
SS&S friendships,
SS&S career paths,
SS&S entertainment,
and even SS&S sleeping.

I invite you to explore SS&S in all aspects of your life. There are two available options for deeper, more advanced training. One is to participate in a webinar that we call, a little tongue-in-cheek, "The Interactive, Post-Graduate Course on the Life-Wide Application of SS&S."

To participate, go to our website, ValuesParenting.com, and find "SS&S Webinars" in the drop-down menu under "Richard and Linda Eyre."

The second option is more intense and personal. We call it "Post-Doctoral, In-Person Small Group SS&S Coaching." These are very selective, small groups that come together at our Park City home for in-depth coaching and training on SS&S living. These weekend sessions are open only to people who have read this book and completed either the SS&S webinar or a private phone conversation with me. For further information, go to the same website. You can also reach me personally or leave any comments through the "Contact Us" link there. I look forward to being in touch and assisting in any way I can with your own personal journey from *paradox* to *paradigm*.

All the best,

Richard M. Eyre

BOOK GROUP
DISCUSSION
QUESTIONS

T*he Happiness Paradox/The Happiness Paradigm* has proven to be a highly stimulating and interactive book for study groups and book groups. Use the questions below along with your own comments and questions to prompt discussion and further probing.

1. Why do you think the author insisted on making this a two-sided book? Does the right-side up and upside-down format add to or detract from the book's message?

2. What was your first impression or reaction when you realized that the author was calling control, ownership, and independence "the three deceivers" and the "joy robbers"? Did you feel like defending these three ideals?

3. As you read further into the book, which of the three deceivers or robbers was hardest to let go of mentally?

4. Did the title of the first side puzzle you or challenge you? When you first read the subtitle, was there even a faint ring of truth in the premise that control, ownership, and independence subtract rather than add to our happiness?

5. Which of the three deceivers did you conclude you had been the most attracted to? Did any of those attractions rise to the level of obsessions? Did you feel that any of them had, at any point in your life, been an addiction?

6. Did you guess or have any ideas about what the three alternatives were before you turned the book over?

7. As you read "The Big Reveal," were the three alternatives surprises to you? Which one initially appealed to you the most? Which one appealed to you least?

8. Was *serendipity* a term you had used or been interested in before reading? What about *stewardship*? Were the words *synergy* and *synchronicity* on your radar? Did combining them make sense in your mind?

9. At what point (if ever) did you begin to feel that it might be worth your time and effort to try to transition from CO&I to SS&S?

10. Were you more interested or less as each of the alternatives were given a spiritual, as well as mental and emotional, direction?

11. Are you interested enough in developing the daily habits of SS&S to try the twenty-one–day exercises the author suggests?

12. If the author were here with you in your book group, what question would you like to ask him?

ACKNOWLEDGMENTS

Thanks to Christopher Robbins, a publisher with a paradigm. His goal is to produce books that celebrate and strengthen family and that embrace and enhance happiness. What he wants to do as a publisher and what I want to do as an author are perfectly matched.

Thanks to David Miles who translates content into compatible, complementing design.

And thanks to Michele Robbins, whose editing forced this book to both higher and deeper levels.

ENDNOTES

1. James Faust, "Our Search for Happiness," *Ensign Magazine,* October 2000, par. 2, https://www.lds.org/ensign/2000/10/ our-search-for-happiness?lang=eng.
2. Pew Research Center, "When Americans Say They Believe in God, What Do They Mean?" April 25, 2019. http://www. pewforum.org/2018/04/25/when-americans-say-they-be-lieve-in-god-what-do-they-mean/.
3. Jon Simpson, "Finding Brand Success in the Digital World," *Forbes,* August 25, 2017, par. 3, https://www. forbes.com/sites/forbesagencycouncil/2017/08/25/ finding-brand-success-in-the-digital-world/#3dc4a60f626e.
4. Matt Ridley, *The Rational Optimist: How Prosperity Evolves* (New York: HarperCollins, 2010), 2.
5. John Robbins, *The New Good Life: Living Better Than Ever in an Age of Less* (New York: Ballantine Books,2010), preface, i.
6. Richard Rohr, *Falling Upward: A Spirituality for the Two Halves of Life* (San Francisco: Jossey-Bass, 2011), preface.
7. "Stewardship (theology)," Wikipedia, last modified October 1, 2018, accessed October 9, 2018, https://en.wikipedia.org/ wiki/Stewardship_(theology).

8. "Synchronicity," Wikipedia, last modified September 22, 2018, accessed October 9, 2018, https://en.wikipedia.org/wiki/Synchronicity.

9. Richard Eyre, *Spiritual Serendipity: Cultivating and Celebrating the Art of the Unexpected* (New York: Simon & Schuster, 1997), 47–51.

10. *Brewer's Dictionary of Phrase and Fable*, Centenary Edition (U.K.: Book Club Associates, 1977), s.v. "Serendipity."

11. Hugh Honour, *Writers and Their Work* (London: F. Mildner & Sons, 1957).

12. Honour, *Writers and Their Work*.

13. Horace Walpole to H. S. Conway, 28 June 1760.

14. Honour, *Writers and Their Work*.

15. Honour, *Writers and Their Work*.

16. Pew Research, "When Americans Say They Believe."

17. G.K. Chesterton, *Orthodoxy* (New York: John Lane Company, 1909), 27.

18. Parley P. Pratt, *Key to the Science of Theology* (Salt Lake City: Deseret Book Co. 10th Edition, 1973), 100.

19. Christopher Howse, "At the Gate of the Year," *Telegraph*, August 16, 2008, https://www.telegraph.co.uk/comment/columnists/christopherhowse/3561497/At-the-Gate-of-the-Year.html.

20. Pratt, *Key to the Science of Theology*, 101.

21. Richard Eyre, *The Thankful Heart* (Sanger: Familius, 2015), back cover.

22. Luke 10:40–41 (Kings James Version).

23. Kristine Maudal and Even Fossen, "Why Going Slow Will Make You Go Faster," *Huffington Post*, April 15, 2018, par. 6, https://www.huffingtonpost.com/kristine-maudal-even-fossen-brainwells/why-going-slow-will-make-you-go-faster_b_7062064.html 4-15-2015.

ABOUT THE AUTHOR

Richard Eyre is the husband of Linda, the father of nine, and the grandfather of thirty-one. His life has been a journey from business and politics to writing and coaching, and from CO&I to SS&S.

ABOUT FAMILIUS

Familius is a publisher dedicated to helping families be happy. We believe that the family is the fundamental unit of society and that happy families are the foundation of a happy life. The greatest work anyone will ever do will be within the walls of his or her own home. And we don't mean vacuuming! We recognize that every family looks different and passionately believe in helping all families find greater joy, whatever their situation. To that end, we publish beautiful books that help families live our 9 Habits of Happy Family Life:

Love Together
Play Together
Learn Together
Work Together
Talk Together
Heal Together
Read Together
Eat Together
Laugh Together

Website: www.familius.com
Facebook: www.facebook.com/paterfamilius
Twitter: @familiustalk, @paterfamilius1
Pinterest: www.pinterest.com/familius

THE MOST IMPORTANT WORK YOU
EVER DO WILL BE WITHIN THE
WALLS OF YOUR OWN HOME.

CPSIA information can be obtained
at www.ICGtesting.com
Printed in the USA
LVHW041917030119
602685LV00003B/3